Money Rebellion I
Flip the System
Kenneth Hughes

Published by KLH Publishing
Pawtucket, Rhode Island

Table of Contents

Introduction: The Game Was Rigged—Until You Learned the Rules

You've been told lies about money your entire life.

They told you wealth was for the lucky ones—the kids born with trust funds, the ones whose parents handed them business cards and stock portfolios. They taught you to see money as scarce, mysterious, and out of reach. They convinced you that financial freedom was a privilege reserved for others, not a skill you could master.

But what if everything you believed about wealth was wrong?

What if the system that seems impossibly complex was actually designed to keep you confused? What if the very people who taught you to fear money were the ones profiting from your ignorance?

Here's the truth they never wanted you to discover:

Wealth is not a birthright. It's a blueprint.

Every millionaire started with the same raw materials you have right now—time, curiosity, and the willingness to learn. The difference isn't luck or family connections. It's knowledge. It's understanding how money really works, not how they told you it works.

This book isn't about getting rich quick or following someone else's success story. This is about something far more powerful—it's about rebellion. A rebellion against the systems that profit from keeping you small, confused, and dependent.

Welcome to the Wealth Rebellion

For generations, financial literacy has been gatekept by institutions that benefit from your confusion. Banks that charge fees you don't understand. Investment firms that profit whether you win or lose. Educational systems that teach you to memorize formulas but never explain how to build actual wealth.

They created a game with rules written in fine print, then convinced you the game was too complicated for people like you to play.

But here's what changes everything: once you understand the rules, you stop being a victim of the system and start becoming its master.

This rebellion begins in your mind. It starts the moment you reject the story that wealth is reserved for others and embrace the truth that financial freedom is a learnable skill. Every chapter in this book is designed to hand you another piece of the puzzle—not just information that sounds smart at dinner parties, but practical knowledge that transforms how you think, act, and build your future.

What This Book Will Do for You

This isn't academic theory. This isn't another book that tells you to "think positive" while offering no real tools. This is a blueprint for financial liberation that meets you exactly where you are.

Whether you're a teenager with no money but big dreams, a creative who's tired of struggling, or anyone who's ever felt left behind by traditional financial advice—this book speaks your language. We'll break down complex concepts using simple analogies. We'll show you how to spot the tricks they use to keep you confused. Most importantly, we'll give you the confidence to take control of your financial destiny.

You'll discover how money really works—not the sanitized version they teach in school, but the raw mechanics of wealth building. You'll learn to see opportunities where others see obstacles. You'll understand how to leverage systems that were designed to work against you and make them work for you instead.

The Promise of Transformation

By the time you finish this book, you won't just have more knowledge about money—you'll have a completely different relationship with it. You'll stop seeing wealth as something that happens to other people and start seeing it as something you create.

You'll learn to think in assets instead of expenses. You'll understand compound interest not as a math concept, but as the closest thing to magic in the financial world. You'll discover funding sources you never knew existed and investment strategies that don't require a finance degree to understand.

Most importantly, you'll join a community of rebels who refuse to accept that financial freedom is reserved for the privileged few. You'll become someone who doesn't just build wealth—you teach others how to build it too.

Your Rebellion Starts Now

Every page you turn is an act of defiance against a system that counted on your ignorance. Every concept you master is a step toward the freedom they told you wasn't meant for people like you.

The game was rigged, but now you know the rules.

The system was designed to exclude you, but now you understand how it works.

They profited from your confusion, but that ends today.

Your wealth rebellion doesn't start when you have money—it starts when you decide that your financial future is too important to leave in someone else's hands. It starts when you choose knowledge over ignorance, action over excuses, and possibility over limitation.

Welcome to the movement that's rewriting the rules of wealth.

Welcome to your rebellion.

Let's flip the system.

Chapter 1: What Money Really Is

> *"Money is not what you think it is. It's not wealth. It's not security. It's not even real in the way most people believe. Money is a story—and whoever controls the story controls your financial future."*

We start here at the first layer of your financial awakening. Everything you thought you knew about money is about to shift. By the end of this chapter, you'll see dollar bills differently. You'll understand why some people get rich while others stay broke, even when they work just as hard. Most importantly, you'll begin to see money not as a mysterious force that controls your life, but as a tool you can learn to master.

The Great Money Illusion

Let me start with a question that might seem obvious: What makes a dollar bill worth a dollar?

Take a moment to really think about it. Pull out a dollar bill if you have one. Look at it. Feel it. What you're holding is a piece of paper with some ink on it. The materials it's made from are worth maybe a few cents. So why can you trade this piece of paper for food, clothes, or a ride across town?

The answer reveals the first truth about money: **Money only works because we all agree it works.**

This is called *fiat currency*—money that has value not because it's made of something precious like gold or silver, but because everyone believes it has value. "Fiat" is Latin for "let it be done," which essentially means "because we said so." Your dollar is worth a dollar because the government says it is, banks accept it as payment, and everyone trusts that others will accept it too.

Think of it like a massive game of make-believe that we all play together. Imagine if tomorrow, everyone decided Monopoly money was real and dollars were fake. Suddenly, your wallet would be worthless, and game boards would make people rich. That's how fragile the entire system really is—it runs on collective trust and agreement.

The Trust Machine

Money is fundamentally a trust system. When you accept payment for your work, you're trusting that other people will accept that same payment when you want to buy something. When you deposit money in a bank, you're trusting they'll give it back. When you invest in a company, you're trusting their leadership to grow your money.

But here's where it gets interesting: some people understand this trust game better than others. They know how to build trust, leverage trust, and sometimes even manipulate trust to their advantage.

Consider this scenario: Two people are selling identical laptops. Person A charges $800 and operates from a fancy store with professional signs and a polished website. Person B charges $600 and operates from their garage with handwritten flyers. Even though the laptops are identical, most people will buy from Person A. Why? Because the fancy store creates more trust, even though the actual product is the same.

This is how perception shapes financial reality. The person who understands how to build trust and credibility can charge more for the same thing. They're not cheating—they're playing the trust game more skillfully.

Value vs. Price: The Hidden Language of Markets

Here's another mind-bending truth: **price and value are not the same thing.**

Value is what something is actually worth to you. *Price* is what someone charges for it. These two things can be wildly different, and understanding this difference is how smart people build wealth.

Let's use a simple analogy. Imagine you're dying of thirst in a desert, and someone offers you a bottle of water for $100. In a grocery store, that bottle costs $1. So what's the "real" price of the water?

The answer is: it depends. In the desert, when your life depends on it, that water might be worth $100 to you. In the grocery store, surrounded by hundreds of identical bottles, it's worth $1. Same water, different circumstances, different value.

Now apply this to everything around you. That iPhone you saved for months to buy? Apple probably spent $400 to make it but charged you $1,200. The difference between the cost and the price is profit—but it's also a measure of how much value Apple convinced you the phone would add to your life.

Smart investors look for situations where the price is lower than the value. They buy things when others don't recognize their worth, then sell them when everyone realizes how valuable they are. It's like being the first person to discover a amazing restaurant before it gets famous—you get the best experience at the lowest price.

The Perception Game

Markets—whether it's the stock market, real estate, or even your local marketplace—are driven by perception more than reality. This creates opportunities for people who learn to see clearly while others react emotionally.

Think of the stock market like a mood ring for millions of people. When investors feel optimistic, prices go up. When they feel scared, prices go down. The actual companies haven't changed overnight, but the collective emotion drives the price.

Here's a real-world example: In 2020, toilet paper didn't become more valuable overnight. The same rolls that cost $10 one week were selling for $50 the next. Did toilet paper suddenly become five times better at its job? No. People's perception of scarcity made them willing to pay more.

Understanding this gives you a massive advantage. While others panic or get swept up in hype, you can ask: "What's really happening here? Is this price reflecting actual value, or just emotion?"

The Simple Analogy That Changes Everything

Imagine money as water flowing through pipes. The pipes represent different financial systems—banks, investments, businesses, markets. Most people stand at the end of one pipe, waiting for drops to fall into their bucket. They work harder, hoping for more drops.

But wealthy people do something different. They don't just catch water—they build more pipes. They create systems that direct water flow toward them from multiple sources. Some build their own pipes (businesses). Others redirect existing flows (investments). The smartest ones figure out how to control where the water goes (they understand the systems that move money around).

The water itself isn't magic. The pipes aren't magic. But understanding how the whole system works? That's the closest thing to magic in the financial world.

Your New Money Reality

By now, your relationship with money should be shifting. You're starting to see it not as a mysterious force, but as a human-created system with rules you can learn and leverage.

Money isn't real in the way a tree or a rock is real. It's a shared story, a collective agreement, a trust system that runs on perception and belief. But here's the beautiful part: once you understand the story, you can start writing your own chapters.

You don't have to be a victim of other people's financial stories. You don't have to accept the prices others set or the limitations they place on what's possible. You can learn to create value, build trust, spot opportunities, and position yourself where the money flows.

The game isn't rigged against you—you just weren't taught the rules. But now you're learning them, one chapter at a time.

Chapter Challenge: See Money Differently

For the next week, practice seeing money as a story rather than a thing:

- When you buy something, ask yourself: "Am I paying for the actual value or for the story they're telling me about this product?"

- Notice how your perception of price changes based on context. How much would you pay for a bottle of water at a gas station versus at a fancy hotel?

- Look for examples where price and value don't match. Maybe it's an underpriced stock, an overpriced coffee, or a service that costs more because of its reputation rather than its quality.

Remember: the goal isn't to become cynical about money, but to become conscious. Once you see money as a tool and a system rather than a master and a mystery, you're ready for the next step in your wealth rebellion.

In the next chapter, we'll explore the mindset that separates people who build wealth from people who just earn money. Because understanding what money is, was just the beginning—now we need to rewire how you think about it.

The revolution in your financial life starts with the revolution in your mind.

Chapter 2: The Wealth Mindset

"Your relationship with money begins in your mind. Change your thoughts, change your bank account. It's not about positive thinking—it's about clear thinking."

We are moving onto the most important chapter in this entire book. Everything else we'll discuss—investments, strategies, systems—will be useless if you skip this foundation. Because here's what the wealthy understand that others miss: building wealth isn't just about what you do with money. It's about how you think about money.

Your mindset is like the operating system of a computer. You can install all the best software in the world, but if your operating system is outdated or corrupted, nothing will work properly. This chapter is about upgrading your mental operating system to one that creates wealth instead of limiting it.

The Great Divide: Scarcity vs. Abundance

Every financial decision you make flows from one of two fundamental beliefs about the world. These beliefs shape how you see opportunities, how you react to setbacks, and ultimately, how much wealth you'll build in your lifetime.

The Scarcity Trap

A scarcity mindset operates from the belief that there's never enough—not enough money, not enough opportunities, not enough time. People trapped in this mindset think like this:

- "I can't afford that" (without exploring ways to make it possible)
- "The rich get richer while the poor get poorer" (seeing wealth as a zero-sum game)
- "I need to save every penny" (hoarding instead of investing)
- "That's too risky" (avoiding all uncertainty, even profitable uncertainty)
- "Money is the root of all evil" (creating internal resistance to wealth)

Here's what's fascinating: scarcity thinking often becomes a self-fulfilling prophecy. When you believe opportunities are rare, you don't look for them. When you believe money is hard to make, you don't pursue income-generating activities. When you believe wealthy people are somehow different from you, you don't study their strategies.

Scarcity mindset isn't about how much money you have—it's about how you think about money. Some people with millions in the bank still operate from scarcity, hoarding wealth instead of growing it. Meanwhile, some people with empty pockets think abundantly and create opportunities others can't see.

The Abundance Revolution

An abundance mindset operates from the belief that wealth can be created, opportunities can be found or made, and there's enough success to go around. People with this mindset think like this:

- "How can I afford that?" (solution-focused rather than limitation-focused)
- "Wealth is created when people solve problems" (seeing money as a byproduct of value creation)
- "I need to invest wisely" (money as a tool for growth, not just security)
- "What's the real risk here?" (calculating risks instead of avoiding them)
- "Money amplifies who you are" (neutral view of wealth as a tool)

This doesn't mean being reckless or unrealistic. Abundance thinking is actually more logical than scarcity thinking because it acknowledges reality: throughout history, humans have consistently created more wealth, more opportunities, and more solutions to problems. The pie keeps getting bigger.

Consider this: every business you interact with daily—from your favorite app to the local coffee shop—exists because someone saw an opportunity where others saw obstacles. They didn't wait for permission or perfect conditions. They operated from abundance, believing they could create value that didn't exist before.

From Expenses to Assets: The Mental Shift That Changes Everything

Most people are taught to think in terms of expenses. They see everything through the lens of "What does this cost?" But wealthy people have rewired their brains to think in terms of assets. They ask, "What does this build?"

Understanding the Asset vs. Expense Mindset

An *expense* takes money out of your pocket and gives you nothing in return except temporary satisfaction or utility. An *asset* puts money into your pocket over time or appreciates in value.

But here's where it gets interesting: the same purchase can be either an expense or an asset, depending on how you use it.

Example 1: The Car

- **Expense mindset**: "This car costs $300 per month in payments plus insurance and gas. It's expensive, but I need it to get to work."
- **Asset mindset**: "This reliable car lets me work rideshare on weekends, earning $200 extra per week. It pays for itself and generates profit."

Example 2: The Course

- **Expense mindset**: "This $500 course is expensive. I could use that money for bills."
- **Asset mindset**: "This course teaches skills that could increase my income by $1,000 per month. It's an investment that pays for itself in two weeks."

Example 3: The Smartphone

- **Expense mindset**: "This phone costs $1,200. That's a lot of money."
- **Asset mindset**: "This phone has professional cameras and editing software. I can use it to start a photography side business or create content that generates income."

The asset mindset doesn't mean buying everything and justifying it as an investment. It means training yourself to see potential where others see only cost. It means asking, "How can I make this thing pay for itself and then some?"

The Asset Accumulation Game

Once you start thinking in assets, you begin playing a completely different game. Instead of just earning money to spend it, you earn money to buy things that make you more money. Instead of trading time for dollars indefinitely, you build systems that generate income with less direct time investment.

This creates what wealthy people call the "asset flywheel":

1. You earn money through work or business
1. You use that money to buy assets (investments, skills, tools, systems)

1. Those assets generate more money

1. You use that new money to buy more assets

1. The cycle accelerates over time

Poor and middle-class people often get stuck in step one forever—earning money just to spend it on expenses that don't generate returns. Wealthy people quickly move to building the flywheel.

Emotional Clarity: The Hidden Superpower

Money triggers powerful emotions—fear, greed, shame, pride, anxiety, excitement. These emotions aren't bad, but they can lead to terrible financial decisions if you don't understand how to work with them.

The Emotional Tax on Wealth Building

Every time you make a financial decision based on emotion instead of logic, you pay what I call an "emotional tax." Here are the most expensive emotional taxes:

Fear Tax: Keeping all your money in low-interest savings accounts because you're afraid to invest. The cost? Decades of missed growth.

Pride Tax: Refusing to ask for help, learn from others, or admit mistakes. The cost? Repeating expensive errors and missing mentorship opportunities.

Instant Gratification Tax: Buying things you want now instead of investing for what you'll need later. The cost? Trading your future wealth for present pleasure.

Perfectionism Tax: Waiting for the "perfect" investment or business opportunity before taking action. The cost? Missing years of potential growth while researching endlessly.

Comparison Tax: Making financial decisions to impress others or keep up with appearances. The cost? Spending money on liabilities instead of assets.

Developing Emotional Intelligence with Money

Emotional clarity doesn't mean suppressing emotions—it means understanding them and not letting them drive your financial decisions. Here's how to build this superpower:

Step 1: Name the Feeling

Before making any significant financial decision, pause and ask: "What am I feeling right now?" Fear? Excitement? Pressure? FOMO? Just naming the emotion reduces its power over you.

Step 2: Separate Feeling from Fact

Ask yourself: "What are the facts here, separate from my emotions?" Write down the actual numbers, risks, and potential outcomes without emotional language.

Step 3: Consider Your Future Self

Ask: "How will the version of me five years from now feel about this decision?" This creates distance from immediate emotions and connects you to long-term consequences.

Step 4: Use the 24-Hour Rule

For any significant financial decision, wait at least 24 hours before acting. This simple pause often prevents expensive emotional decisions.

Long-Term Vision: Your North Star

One of the biggest differences between wealthy and non-wealthy people is time horizon. Poor financial decisions are often made with a short-term perspective. Great financial decisions are made with a long-term vision.

The Power of Playing the Long Game

When you have a clear vision of where you want to be financially in 10, 20, or 30 years, current decisions become much easier. That expensive coffee every day stops looking like a small expense and starts looking like $1,800 per year that could be invested. That side hustle stops looking like extra work and starts looking like the foundation of your future business empire.

Long-term vision also helps you stay motivated during difficult periods. Building wealth isn't always exciting. Sometimes it's boring. Sometimes it requires sacrifice. But when you're connected to your future vision, you can endure temporary discomfort for permanent improvement.

Creating Your Wealth Vision

Take some time to envision your ideal financial future. Not just "I want to be rich," but specifically:

- What does financial freedom look like for your daily life?
- What opportunities would you pursue if money wasn't a constraint?
- How would you contribute to your family, community, or causes you care about?
- What legacy do you want to build?

Write this vision down. Make it vivid. Make it personal. This becomes your North Star—the fixed point that guides your financial decisions when emotions try to pull you off course.

The Compound Effect of Right Thinking

Here's what most people don't realize: your mindset compounds just like your investments. Every time you choose abundance over scarcity, assets over expenses, clarity over emotion, and long-term over short-term, you're not just making one good decision. You're strengthening the mental patterns that will guide thousands of future decisions.

A person with a wealth mindset doesn't just make one good investment—they develop the thinking patterns that help them spot opportunities consistently. They don't just save money once—they build systems that make wise financial choices automatic.

This is why mindset work isn't soft or optional. It's the foundation that determines whether all your other wealth-building efforts succeed or fail.

Your Mindset Rebellion Starts Now

The old you might have thought wealthy people were just lucky or different. The new you understands that wealth starts with a decision to think differently about money, opportunities, and your own potential.

The old you might have seen every purchase as an expense. The new you will start seeing investments, assets, and income-generating potential everywhere.

The old you might have been driven by fear and short-term thinking. The new you will make decisions based on clarity and long-term vision.

This isn't about fake positivity or pretending you have money when you don't. This is about rewiring your mental operating system to one that creates wealth instead of limiting it.

Chapter Challenge: Mindset Audit

For the next week, pay attention to your automatic thoughts about money:

1. **Track Your Language**: Notice when you say things like "I can't afford it" vs. "How could I afford it?" The language you use shapes how you think.

1. **Identify Your Emotional Triggers**: What financial situations make you feel anxious, angry, or impulsive? Awareness is the first step to emotional clarity.

1. **Practice Asset Thinking**: Before making any purchase over $50, ask yourself: "Is this an expense or could this be an asset? How might I use this to generate income or value?"

1. **Connect to Your Future**: Spend 10 minutes writing about your ideal financial future. Get specific. Get excited. Get connected to your long-term vision.

Remember: your current financial situation is the result of your past thinking patterns. Your future financial situation will be the result of the thinking patterns you choose starting now.

In the next chapter, we'll explore how to maintain this wealth mindset when the world around you tries to pull you back into scarcity thinking. Because building wealth isn't just about changing your mind once—it's about protecting and strengthening that mindset every single day.

Your rebellion against limitation begins in your mind. Let the transformation continue.

Chapter 3: Maintaining the Wealth Mindset

"Building a wealth mindset is revolutionary. Protecting it daily? That's where true rebellion lives. Your mind is your most valuable asset—guard it like the treasure it is."

You've begun to understand what money really is. You've started rewiring your thoughts from scarcity to abundance, from expenses to assets. But here's what separates the dreamers from the builders: consistency. Anyone can adopt a wealth mindset for a day, a week, or even a month. The true rebels learn how to maintain it when life gets messy, when doubt creeps in, and when the world tries to pull them back into old patterns.

This chapter is your fortress-building manual—the blueprint for creating unshakable mental wealth that compounds over time. Because in a world designed to keep you financially confused and emotionally reactive, protecting your peace isn't just self-care. It's your most powerful wealth-building strategy.

The Daily Architecture of Wealthy Thinking

Your mindset isn't built in grand moments—it's crafted in the quiet minutes between sunrise and the world's demands. Wealthy people understand this truth: daily habits create mental patterns, and mental patterns create financial outcomes.

Morning Mind Programming

The first thirty minutes of your day set the tone for every financial decision that follows. During this precious window, your mind is most receptive to new programming, free from the day's chaos and external influences.

The Wealth Morning Ritual:

Minutes 1-10: Gratitude and Abundance Scanning

Begin each day by acknowledging three things you're grateful for—but make them specific to your financial journey. Instead of generic gratitude, focus on opportunities, resources, or progress that connects to your wealth-building vision.

- "I'm grateful for the side project that earned me $200 this month"
- "I appreciate having a reliable internet connection that lets me learn and work remotely"
- "I'm thankful for the friend who introduced me to investing concepts"

This practice trains your brain to scan for abundance and opportunity rather than lack and limitation.

Minutes 11-20: Future Self Visualization

Close your eyes and spend time with the financially free version of yourself. Don't just imagine having money—experience the feelings, choices, and daily reality of someone who has mastered wealth creation. What does their morning routine look like? How do they make decisions? What opportunities do they pursue?

This isn't fantasy—it's mental rehearsal. Athletes visualize perfect performances before competitions. Musicians imagine flawless concerts before taking the stage. You're programming your subconscious to recognize and pursue wealth-building opportunities.

Minutes 21-30: Intention Setting

End your morning ritual by setting one specific financial intention for the day. Not a massive goal, but a single action aligned with your wealth vision:

- "Today I'll research one new investment opportunity"
- "I'll track my expenses to understand my spending patterns"
- "I'll reach out to someone who could mentor me or collaborate with me"

Mental Detox: Clearing the Noise

Just as you shower daily to clean your body, you need daily practices to clean your mind of the mental pollution that accumulates from living in a financially confused world.

Information Diet Audit

Most people consume financial poison daily without realizing it. Social media feeds filled with luxury purchases they can't afford. News focused on economic doom and scarcity. Conversations with people who complain about money but never study it.

Conduct a weekly audit of your information diet:

- What financial messages are you absorbing through social media?
- Which news sources are feeding you fear-based financial content?
- What conversations are reinforcing limiting beliefs about money?

Replace toxic inputs with nourishing ones:

- Follow accounts that share wealth-building education, not lifestyle envy

- Read books and articles that expand your financial understanding

- Listen to podcasts featuring people who've built wealth from similar starting points as yours

The Evening Mental Reset

Before sleep, spend five minutes clearing your mind of the day's financial stress or confusion. Write down any money-related worries, then beside each worry, write one small action you could take tomorrow to address it.

This practice prevents financial anxiety from disrupting your sleep while training your brain to focus on solutions rather than problems.

Circle Audits: The People Who Shape Your Financial Future

Show me your five closest friends, and I'll predict your financial future with startling accuracy. This isn't about judgment—it's about recognizing that beliefs are contagious, and the people around you heavily influence your relationship with money.

The Influence Inventory

Create three lists of people in your life:

The Elevators: People who inspire you to think bigger, challenge limiting beliefs, and share resources or opportunities. They don't have to be wealthy, but they must be growth-minded and supportive of your financial goals.

The Neutrals: People who neither help nor hinder your wealth-building journey. They're good friends or family members, but money isn't something you discuss or learn from them about.

The Drainers: People who consistently reinforce scarcity thinking, discourage your growth efforts, or pull you into spending money on things that don't align with your goals.

Be honest about these categories. Someone can be a wonderful person and still be financially toxic for your journey.

Strategic Relationship Building

Once you've completed your circle audit, make strategic adjustments:

Minimize Time with Drainers: This doesn't mean cutting people out of your life, but it means being intentional about when and how you engage. If your coworkers constantly complain about money during lunch, eat at your desk while reading something educational. If family gatherings always include pressure to spend money you don't have, prepare responses in advance and stick to your budget.

Maximize Learning from Elevators: Seek out more time with people who expand your financial thinking. Ask them questions about their money strategies. Share your goals and ask for feedback. Most successful people love helping others who are serious about growth.

Find Your Financial Community: If your current circle lacks wealth-minded people, actively seek them out. Join investment clubs, attend entrepreneurship meetups, participate in online communities focused on financial education. The internet has made it easier than ever to connect with like-minded people who will support your financial growth.

Emotional Discipline: Your Wealth Defense System

Money is emotional. Every financial decision carries the weight of fears, dreams, past experiences, and future hopes. Learning to make decisions from clarity rather than emotion is perhaps the most valuable skill you can develop.

The Emotional Weather Forecast

Start paying attention to your emotional states the way a pilot watches weather patterns. Certain emotions create financial turbulence that leads to poor decisions:

Storm Warning Emotions:

- **Anxiety**: Often leads to selling investments too early or avoiding calculated risks
- **FOMO (Fear of Missing Out)**: Causes impulsive purchases or chasing trending investments
- **Pride**: Prevents you from asking for help or admitting mistakes
- **Shame**: Makes you avoid dealing with financial problems or learning from failures
- **Comparison**: Drives spending to keep up with others rather than building your own wealth

Calm Weather Emotions:

- **Curiosity**: Opens you to learning and exploring new opportunities
- **Confidence**: Helps you take calculated risks and stick to your plans
- **Contentment**: Prevents impulse purchases and helps you appreciate what you have
- **Excitement tempered with patience**: Motivates action while maintaining long-term perspective

The 24-Hour Financial Decision Rule

For any significant financial decision—whether it's an investment, major purchase, or business opportunity—implement a mandatory 24-hour waiting period. During this time:

1. **Name the emotion** driving your desire to act

1. **Research the facts** without emotional language

1. **Consider the opportunity cost** of this decision

1. **Ask your future self** how they'd feel about this choice in five years

This simple practice prevents the majority of emotional financial mistakes while ensuring you don't miss genuinely good opportunities.

Resilience Rituals: Bouncing Back from Financial Setbacks

Building wealth isn't a straight line. You'll face setbacks, make mistakes, and encounter unexpected challenges. The difference between those who eventually succeed and those who give up isn't the absence of problems—it's the presence of resilience rituals that help them recover quickly.

The Setback Recovery Protocol:

Step 1: Acknowledge Without Judgment (24 hours)

When something goes wrong financially—you lose money on an investment, a business idea fails, you make an impulse purchase—give yourself 24 hours to feel disappointed without trying to fix or analyze anything. This prevents emotional decisions made in reaction to setbacks.

Step 2: Extract the Learning (48 hours)

After the initial emotional response has passed, write down what you learned from the experience. What information did you miss? What emotional triggers influenced your decision? What would you do differently? Every setback becomes valuable if it teaches you something.

Step 3: Adjust and Act (72 hours)

Within 72 hours of any financial setback, take one small positive action toward your wealth-building goals. This could be as simple as reading an article about investing, updating your budget, or reaching out to someone for advice. The key is to prevent setbacks from creating momentum in the wrong direction.

Protecting Your Peace: The Ultimate Financial Strategy

In a world that profits from your anxiety, confusion, and impulsive decisions, protecting your mental peace isn't just good for your well-being—it's a competitive advantage. When you operate from calm clarity instead of reactive emotion, you make better decisions, spot opportunities others miss, and build wealth more efficiently.

The Peace Protection Framework

Boundary Setting with Financial Stress

Create clear boundaries around when and how you engage with financial information:

- Set specific times for checking investments, not constantly throughout the day
- Designate certain days as "money-free" where you don't think about finances
- Choose one day per week for financial planning and decision-making

Environmental Design for Clarity

Your physical environment influences your mental state. Create spaces that support clear financial thinking:

- Keep a dedicated area free from distractions for financial planning
- Remove tempting apps from your phone's home screen
- Surround yourself with visual reminders of your long-term goals rather than short-term desires

Energy Management Over Time Management

Protect your mental energy for the financial decisions that matter most. Make routine financial tasks automatic through systems and habits, so your brainpower is available for strategic thinking and opportunity recognition.

The Compound Effect of Consistent Practice

Here's what most people miss: maintaining a wealth mindset isn't just about avoiding bad financial decisions. It's about creating the mental conditions where good opportunities naturally gravitate toward you.

When you consistently operate from abundance rather than scarcity, you become someone others want to do business with. When you maintain emotional clarity, you spot trends and opportunities that stressed people miss. When you protect your peace, you have the mental space to think creatively about wealth creation.

Every day you maintain these practices, you're not just strengthening your mindset—you're compounding your ability to build wealth. Like interest on money, consistency of thought creates exponential returns over time.

Your Daily Rebellion Against Limitation

Maintaining a wealth mindset in a scarcity-focused world is an act of daily rebellion. Every morning you choose abundance thinking over fear-based media consumption, you rebel. Every time you make financial decisions from clarity rather than emotion, you rebel. Every moment you protect your mental peace from external chaos, you rebel.

This isn't passive resistance—it's active creation. You're not just rejecting the old patterns; you're building new ones. You're not just avoiding financial traps; you're creating wealth-building habits.

Chapter Challenge: Your 30-Day Mindset Maintenance Plan

For the next 30 days, commit to these daily practices:

Morning (10 minutes):

- 3 specific abundance-focused gratitudes
- 5 minutes of future self visualization
- Set one small financial intention for the day

Evening (5 minutes):

- Write down any financial worries and one action to address each
- Review one thing you learned about money or wealth-building today

Weekly (30 minutes):

- Audit your information diet and make one improvement
- Evaluate your circle's influence on your financial thinking
- Plan one action to connect with wealth-minded people

Monthly:

- Complete a full circle audit
- Assess your emotional patterns around money
- Adjust your peace protection strategies based on what's working

Track your progress not just in dollars earned or saved, but in mental clarity, emotional stability, and the quality of opportunities that come your way. You'll be amazed at how maintaining your wealth mindset creates wealth in ways you never expected.

Remember: Your mind is your most valuable asset. Everything else you build flows from the thoughts you think and the mental patterns you maintain. Guard your mindset like the treasure it is, because in the game of wealth building, the person with the clearest thinking always wins.

In our next chapter, we'll explore how to translate this rock-solid mindset into unconventional paths to wealth—opportunities that exist all around you but are invisible to people trapped in traditional thinking. Your mental foundation is strong. Now let's build your financial empire.

The revolution continues in your daily choices. **Keep rebelling.**

Chapter 4: The Power of Compound Interest

"The most powerful force in the universe is compound interest." — Albert Einstein

Discover the power of compound interest, a key to building wealth. This chapter explores this concept, not just as a formula, but as a testament to the impact of time, patience, and consistent effort.

As we journey together into this exploration, I invite you to see compound interest as a quiet rebellion against the idea that wealth is only for the few. It is a universal law that works for anyone, regardless of their starting point. It is the great equalizer, a silent partner that labors for you day and night, turning small, consistent efforts into a legacy of abundance. May this chapter inspire you to harness this incredible force and begin building a future of true financial sovereignty.

Understanding Compound Interest

At its heart, compound interest is a simple idea: it is the interest you earn on your initial investment, plus the interest you earn on the accumulated interest. Think of it as a snowball rolling down a hill. It starts small, but as it rolls, it picks up more snow, growing larger and faster. Your money works in the same way. The earnings your investment generates are reinvested, and those reinvested earnings begin to generate their own earnings. This creates a cycle of accelerating growth.

This is fundamentally different from simple interest, which is calculated only on the principal amount. Simple interest is linear growth—a straight line. Compound interest is exponential growth—a curve that sweeps dramatically upward over time. This exponential nature is what makes it such a powerful tool for building wealth. It transforms your money from a static resource into a dynamic force, a self-perpetuating engine of prosperity.

The beauty of compound interest lies in its accessibility. It does not require a large initial sum or specialized knowledge. Its primary ingredients are time and consistency. By understanding this principle, you are equipping yourself with one of the most effective strategies for flipping the system from one of perpetual work to one of financial freedom, where your money begins to work for you.

Starting Early: The Magic of Time

The most critical element in the compound interest equation is time. The longer your money has to grow, the more powerful the compounding effect becomes. This is because each cycle of interest is added to a larger and larger base, causing the growth to accelerate. Starting early, even with small amounts, can lead to vastly different outcomes than starting later with larger sums.

Let's explore this with a simple story. Imagine two friends, Alex and Ben.

- **Alex** begins investing at age 25. He puts just $100 per month into an account that earns an average of 8% per year. He does this consistently for 10 years and then stops contributing altogether, letting his investment continue to grow. By age 35, he has invested a total of $12,000.

- **Ben** waits to start investing until he is 35. He also invests $100 per month into an account earning 8% per year. He continues to invest this amount every month until he is 65—a total of 30 years. Ben invests a total of $36,000.

When they both retire at age 65, who do you think has more money?

Even though Ben invested three times as much money for three times as long, Alex's account is worth more. By retirement, Alex's initial $12,000 investment has grown to over $213,000. Ben's $36,000 investment has grown to just over $150,000.

This is the power of a 10-year head start. The time Alex's money had to compound created a much larger snowball of wealth. This example is not just a financial lesson; it is a call to action. The best time to start investing was yesterday. The second-best time is today. Every day you wait is a day you lose the powerful ally of time.

Strategies for Maximizing Growth

Harnessing the full potential of compound interest requires more than just understanding the concept. It requires intentional strategies that create an environment for your money to grow as efficiently as possible. Here are a few practical ways to put this force to work for you.

Reinvest All Earnings

The engine of compound interest is reinvestment. To truly benefit, you must ensure that any dividends, interest, or capital gains your investments generate are automatically reinvested back into your account. Many investment platforms and retirement accounts offer a Dividend Reinvestment Plan (DRIP). Activating this feature is one of the simplest and most powerful actions you can take. It ensures your "snowball" is constantly growing and that your earnings start earning their own earnings without any extra effort from you.

Automate Your Contributions

Consistency is key. The easiest way to remain consistent is to remove the need for willpower or daily decision-making. Set up automatic monthly or bi-weekly contributions from your bank account to your investment accounts. Treat this contribution like any other bill—a non-negotiable payment to your future self. Even a small, automated amount invested consistently over time will grow into a substantial sum, thanks to the relentless work of compounding.

Choose High-Yield Accounts and Investments

The rate of return on your investment significantly impacts how quickly your money compounds. While all savings can benefit from compounding, the effect is more dramatic in accounts with higher potential returns.

- **High-Yield Savings Accounts:** For your emergency fund or short-term savings, a high-yield savings account offers a better return than a traditional savings account, allowing your cash to grow faster while remaining safe and accessible.

- **Index Funds and ETFs:** For long-term goals, low-cost index funds or Exchange-Traded Funds (ETFs) that track broad market indexes (like the S&P 500) offer a powerful way to achieve diversified growth. Historically, these investments have delivered average annual returns that far outpace traditional savings accounts, supercharging the compounding process.

- **Retirement Accounts:** Tax-advantaged accounts like a 401(k) or a Roth IRA are excellent vehicles for compounding. Your investments grow tax-deferred or tax-free, allowing the full amount to be reinvested without being diminished by annual taxes.

Overcoming Common Barriers

While the concept of compound interest is simple, putting it into practice can be challenging. Many of us face real-world barriers that can feel overwhelming. Let's address these challenges with compassion and practical solutions.

The Barrier of Debt

High-interest debt, such as from credit cards, works like compound interest in reverse. It grows exponentially against you. It is crucial to have a plan to tackle this debt. Consider strategies like the "debt snowball" (paying off smallest debts first for psychological wins) or the "debt avalanche" (paying off highest-interest debts first to save money). It can be wise to balance paying down high-interest debt with making small, consistent investments. You do not have to wait until you are completely debt-free to start your investment journey.

The Barrier of Procrastination

The story of Alex and Ben shows that the biggest enemy of compound interest is delay. Procrastination often stems from feeling overwhelmed or fearing that you don't know enough. The solution is to start small. You don't need to be an expert to open an investment account and automate a $25 monthly contribution into an index fund. The act of starting, no matter how small, breaks the inertia and begins the compounding process.

The Barrier of Financial Literacy

Feeling like you don't know enough is a common and valid concern. The financial world can seem complex and intimidating. But you do not need a degree in finance to harness compound interest. Begin by reading a few trusted books (like this one!), following reputable financial educators online, or using user-friendly investment apps that simplify the process. Your knowledge will grow alongside your investments.

The Compound Effect on Life

The principle of compounding extends far beyond finance. It is a universal law that applies to every area of your life. The small, seemingly insignificant choices you make every day compound over time to create who you become.

- **Knowledge:** Reading for just 15 minutes a day doesn't seem like much, but over a year, it adds up to dozens of books and a vast expansion of your understanding.

- **Health:** Choosing to walk instead of drive, or eating one healthy meal a day, can compound into significant long-term health benefits, preventing chronic disease and increasing vitality.

- **Relationships:** A small, daily act of kindness or appreciation toward a loved one compounds into a deep, resilient, and trusting bond over the years.

- **Skills:** Practicing a new skill for just 30 minutes each day leads to mastery over time. The small improvements you make each session build upon one another until you achieve a level of proficiency you once thought impossible.

Just as with finance, the compound effect in life is powered by consistency and time. The daily habits you cultivate, for better or for worse, will define your future. By understanding this, you can become a conscious architect of your life, intentionally choosing the small actions that will compound into the future you desire.

Your journey to financial independence is no different. It begins with one small, brave step: making your first investment. That single act, repeated consistently, unleashes the most powerful force in the financial universe. It is your personal rebellion against a system of instant gratification, a quiet commitment to the long-term vision of a life lived in freedom and abundance. You have the knowledge. You have the power. The time to begin is now.

Chapter 5: Negotiate Everything: Reclaiming Value in Every Conversation

> *"If you don't ask, the system wins. If you ask well, you rewrite the rules. Every conversation contains the seeds of transformation, waiting for someone bold enough to plant them, patient enough to nurture them, and strategic enough to harvest their full potential."*

Unlock financial sovereignty through the art of negotiation. This chapter transforms negotiation from a confrontation into a graceful exchange that respects your worth and the dignity of others, impacting all aspects of life where value and mutual benefit can be found.

As we venture together through these transformative pages, I invite you to release any preconceptions about negotiation as aggressive manipulation or desperate pleading. Instead, embrace this ancient art as what it truly represents: the diplomatic bridge between what is and what becomes possible, the respectful conversation that elevates all parties when approached with wisdom, authenticity, and strategic grace.

This chapter serves as your comprehensive guide to reclaiming value in every conversation while nurturing relationships that support your long-term prosperity and personal integrity. Together, we shall explore the psychological foundations that transform negotiation from anxiety-inducing ordeal into confident expression of your inherent worth, develop tactical approaches that create harmonious outcomes, and cultivate the inner preparation that ensures every negotiation serves your highest good.

Negotiation as Rebellion: The Power to Rewrite Reality

In the grand theater of modern commerce and social exchange, we have been conditioned to accept the first offer, the standard terms, the established prices as immutable laws of nature. This conditioning serves those who profit from our compliance while keeping us trapped in a cycle of passive acceptance that diminishes our capacity to create the lives we truly desire.

Your negotiation rebellion begins with a profound recognition: every initial offer represents not a final decree, but an invitation to engage in the sacred dance of value creation. When you negotiate with skill and integrity, you refuse to participate in your own diminishment while creating space for outcomes that serve the genuine interests of all involved parties.

This rebellion acknowledges that flexibility exists in virtually every system, hidden behind policies and procedures designed to discourage exploration. Organizations routinely build adjustment margins into their structures while training representatives to present initial terms as non-negotiable, knowing that most people will accept these limitations without question.

The Mythology of Fixed Prices

The illusion of non-negotiable terms represents one of the most profitable myths in our modern world. Rental properties maintain flexibility to avoid vacancy costs, medical billing systems accommodate financial hardship through payment plans, and financial institutions possess discretionary authority far beyond what their policies might suggest. Understanding this reality transforms you from passive price-taker into active value-creator.

Consider the profound truth that every successful business operates with margins that allow for adjustment. They anticipate negotiation in their pricing structures while hoping you won't recognize this fundamental dynamic. Your awareness of this hidden flexibility becomes your pathway to better terms, improved service, and arrangements that truly serve your needs.

The system counts on your ignorance, your discomfort with advocacy, your willingness to accept whatever terms are initially presented. When you develop negotiation skills, you step outside this carefully constructed paradigm and into a realm where mutual benefit becomes possible through respectful but persistent exploration of alternatives.

Emotional Sovereignty in Negotiation

Effective negotiation requires emotional clarity that separates your inherent worth from the specific outcomes of individual conversations. This distinction prevents the internal collapse that occurs when rejection feels like personal judgment rather than simple business decision, enabling you to maintain strategic thinking even when initial responses suggest inflexibility.

Your emotional sovereignty means approaching every negotiation from a position of inner abundance rather than desperate scarcity. You recognize that multiple solutions exist for every challenge and that today's "no" often transforms into tomorrow's "yes" when circumstances evolve or new information emerges through patient persistence and creative problem-solving.

This foundation of emotional stability enables you to advocate confidently for terms that serve your legitimate interests while remaining open to alternatives that achieve your objectives through different pathways. You become unshakable in your commitment to fair value while remaining flexible about the specific mechanisms through which that value might be realized.

The Sacred Art of Tactical Silence

In our world of constant communication and immediate responses, the strategic use of silence becomes one of your most powerful tools. This deliberate pause creates space for reflection, applies gentle pressure for improved offers, and demonstrates the quiet confidence that comes from being comfortable with temporary uncertainty.

Tactical silence acknowledges a fundamental truth: the person who speaks first after a significant pause often reveals additional information, offers concessions, or provides alternative solutions that would never emerge if the conversation continued at its natural pace. This dynamic works because silence triggers psychological responses that encourage elaboration and creative thinking.

The beauty of strategic silence lies in its respectful nature. Unlike aggressive tactics that create adversarial dynamics, thoughtful pauses are interpreted as careful consideration rather than rejection. This approach maintains the collaborative spirit necessary for long-term relationship building while creating the space necessary for optimal outcomes to emerge.

The Psychology of Pause

When you introduce strategic silence into a negotiation, you create a psychological vacuum that human nature seeks to fill. Most people interpret this pause as contemplation rather than resistance, assuming you're seriously considering their offer while potentially identifying areas that might require adjustment to secure your agreement.

This interpretation encourages them to provide additional information, better terms, or alternative solutions without any pressure or manipulation on your part. They simply respond to the natural human tendency to elaborate when met with thoughtful silence, often revealing flexibility that wasn't initially apparent in their presentation.

Strategic pauses also provide you with invaluable processing time that enables more thoughtful responses while preventing the impulsive agreements that occur when pressure and timing combine to override careful consideration. This breathing space protects you from decisions that might not serve your long-term interests while creating opportunities for creative solutions to emerge.

Implementing Strategic Silence

The power pause immediately following any offer creates space for additional information to emerge while demonstrating your thoughtful approach to important decisions. Rather than immediately accepting or rejecting, you allow the natural weight of the moment to encourage further explanation or improvement of terms.

Consider implementing contemplative silence after questions like "Is that your best offer?" or "What flexibility do you have?" These pauses apply gentle pressure while maintaining a respectful tone that encourages collaboration rather than confrontation in finding solutions that serve everyone's interests.

Processing pauses when presented with complex terms or multiple options demonstrate due diligence while providing psychological permission for the other party to offer clarification, simplification, or enhancement that makes agreement more likely and more favorable to your needs.

Reframing Rejection: Data, Not Defeat

One of the greatest obstacles to effective negotiation lies in our interpretation of "no" as personal rejection rather than valuable information about timing, approach, or alternative pathways that might lead to successful outcomes through modified requests or different strategies.

Every rejection contains precious data about constraints, priorities, and decision-making processes that inform future approaches while revealing opportunities for creative solutions that address the underlying concerns preventing agreement on your original request.

This reframe transforms negotiation from single-attempt transactions into ongoing relationships where today's "no" provides intelligence for tomorrow's more successful approach while building credibility and rapport that support future negotiations and collaborative problem-solving.

The Intelligence Within Refusal

Initial rejections often mask limited authority rather than absolute inflexibility, revealing that the person you're speaking with lacks decision-making power while potentially being sympathetic to your request. This information guides you toward appropriate decision-makers who possess the authority to provide the accommodation you seek.

Timing-based rejections indicate seasonal, cyclical, or procedural constraints that suggest alternative windows when the same request might receive favorable consideration. Understanding these rhythms enables you to align your requests with optimal timing that maximizes your chances of success.

Resource-based rejections reveal budget limitations or competing priorities that might be addressed through modified requests, payment plans, or alternative value propositions that achieve your objectives while accommodating the legitimate constraints faced by the other party.

Converting "No" into Strategic Advantage

Transform rejection into intelligence by asking questions like "What would need to change for this to become possible?" or "When might circumstances be more favorable for this type of request?" These inquiries reveal pathways to future success while maintaining positive relationships that support ongoing collaboration.

Explore alternatives through questions such as "If not this, what options do you have?" or "What similar solutions have worked for others?" This approach often uncovers creative alternatives that achieve your objectives through different mechanisms while demonstrating your flexibility and collaborative spirit.

Build relationships through gracious acceptance of initial rejection while expressing continued interest in finding mutually beneficial solutions. This response creates goodwill and positions you favorably for future opportunities when circumstances change or new possibilities emerge through evolving business needs.

What You Can Negotiate: Expanding Your Awareness

The scope of negotiable elements in modern life extends far beyond obvious candidates like salary and major purchases to encompass virtually every recurring expense, service agreement, and relationship dynamic that affects your financial well-being and personal satisfaction.

This expanded awareness transforms routine interactions into opportunities for value optimization while building negotiation skills through low-stakes practice that prepares you for high-impact conversations involving substantial financial implications and long-term relationship consequences.

Understanding negotiation opportunities requires shifting from passive acceptance of standard terms to active curiosity about alternatives that might provide better value, improved service, or more favorable conditions aligned with your specific needs and circumstances.

Housing and Living Expenses

Your largest monthly expense—housing—contains numerous negotiable elements beyond the obvious rental rate. Lease terms, security deposits, pet policies, maintenance responsibilities, and renewal conditions can all be adjusted to significantly impact your total housing costs while improving your living experience through customized arrangements.

Property managers often possess discretionary authority that extends far beyond their initial presentations, particularly when faced with quality tenants who demonstrate reliability and care for the property. Your track record as a responsible occupant becomes valuable currency in these conversations.

Utility negotiations with service providers frequently yield reduced rates through budget billing plans, energy efficiency programs, or competitive retention offers designed to prevent customer defection. These conversations require minimal time investment while potentially generating substantial monthly savings that compound over years of residency.

Medical and Healthcare Costs

Healthcare represents one of the most negotiable expense categories, though many people never realize the flexibility that exists within these systems. Medical billing departments routinely negotiate payment plans and reductions for patients facing financial hardship, while insurance companies maintain appeals processes that frequently result in coverage for initially denied treatments.

Prescription drug costs can often be reduced through manufacturer assistance programs, generic alternatives, and pharmacy price matching that requires awareness of available options and willingness to research alternatives that provide equivalent therapeutic outcomes at substantially reduced costs.

Elective procedures and specialist services frequently offer package deals, cash discounts, or payment plans that reduce total costs while making necessary healthcare more accessible through creative financing arrangements that benefit both patients and providers.

Financial Services and Banking

Financial institutions operate with far more flexibility than their standardized fee schedules might suggest. Credit card interest rates respond to payment history and competitive offers, while retention departments possess authority to provide rate reductions that aren't advertised but become available when customers demonstrate willingness to consider alternative providers.

Bank fees often disappear when challenged respectfully, as customer service representatives maintain discretionary power to waive charges for account holders who demonstrate value through relationship longevity and account activity. These conversations typically require minimal time while potentially saving hundreds of dollars annually.

Loan terms including interest rates, payment schedules, and fees contain flexibility that emerges through competitive shopping and skilled negotiation. Refinancing opportunities create leverage for improved terms on existing obligations, particularly when you demonstrate creditworthiness and alternative options.

Employment and Income Negotiations

Professional negotiations extend far beyond base salary to encompass benefits, flexible work arrangements, professional development opportunities, and performance incentives that can significantly increase total compensation while improving job satisfaction and career development prospects.

Freelance and contract negotiations involve rates, payment terms, scope definitions, and intellectual property rights that affect both immediate compensation and long-term value creation. These discussions establish the foundation for professional relationships that support ongoing income generation and career advancement.

Understanding your market value through research and competitive analysis provides objective basis for compensation discussions while demonstrating professional approach that respects both parties' interests in fair and competitive arrangements reflecting current market conditions and individual contribution.

Ninja Tactics: Advanced Negotiation Strategies

Mastering negotiation requires understanding psychological principles and tactical approaches that create favorable conditions for agreement while maintaining respectful relationships that support long-term success and collaborative problem-solving in future interactions.

These advanced strategies align with natural human psychology and decision-making patterns while creating value for all parties through creative solutions that address underlying needs rather than stated positions that may mask more fundamental interests.

Implementation of these sophisticated techniques requires practice and emotional regulation that enables strategic thinking under pressure while maintaining authenticity and integrity that builds rather than undermines trust and mutual respect between negotiating parties.

Anchoring and Concession Strategies

High anchoring establishes reference points that influence subsequent negotiations by creating context for what seems reasonable while providing room for concessions that still achieve favorable outcomes compared to your minimum acceptable terms. This psychological principle works because initial numbers significantly influence perception of subsequent offers.

Strategic concessions that appear significant but cost little create goodwill while maintaining momentum toward agreement. These carefully planned accommodations trigger reciprocity psychology that encourages matching concessions from the other party in pursuit of mutually satisfactory outcomes.

Conditional offers that tie concessions to corresponding benefits prevent one-sided accommodation while ensuring that any flexibility you demonstrate results in improved terms rather than simply reducing your position without reciprocal consideration from the other party.

Question-Based Influence

Open-ended questions reveal valuable information about constraints, priorities, and decision-making processes while encouraging collaborative problem-solving that finds solutions within available parameters rather than demanding impossible accommodations that create adversarial dynamics.

Assumptive questions that presume agreement on basic principles while exploring implementation details create momentum toward resolution while identifying specific obstacles that need addressing for successful agreement between all parties involved.

Alternative-generating questions that explore multiple solutions create abundance mindset while preventing fixation on single options that may not be achievable under current circumstances but have viable alternatives that serve similar purposes and meet underlying needs.

Timing and Leverage Optimization

End-of-period negotiations leverage quota pressures and budget cycles while providing motivation for decision-makers to offer concessions that clear inventory, meet targets, or utilize available resources before deadlines that might otherwise result in lost opportunities for mutual benefit.

Market timing that coincides with competitive pressures or industry changes creates urgency while providing external reasons for accommodation that don't depend solely on your persuasive abilities but align with broader business incentives and organizational objectives.

Personal timing that considers your own alternatives and constraints prevents desperation while ensuring you negotiate from strength rather than weakness that undermines your position and reduces likelihood of achieving favorable outcomes that serve your long-term interests.

Sacred Rituals for Negotiation Mastery

Effective negotiation requires internal preparation that aligns your energy, clarifies your intentions, and builds the emotional foundation necessary for confident communication while maintaining flexibility to recognize and accept alternatives that serve your interests.

These preparation rituals create the mental and emotional space necessary for strategic thinking while preventing reactive responses that undermine negotiation effectiveness through premature concessions or aggressive behaviors that damage relationships and compromise future opportunities.

Regular practice of these centering techniques builds negotiation confidence while developing the internal resources necessary for persistent advocacy that achieves favorable outcomes without compromising personal integrity or professional relationships that support long-term success.

Breathwork for Negotiation Confidence

Pre-negotiation breathing exercises center your energy while reducing anxiety that might interfere with clear thinking and confident communication during important conversations that affect your financial well-being and professional relationships. These simple techniques create immediate access to calm confidence.

Practice confidence breathing that emphasizes strong, controlled exhales to release tension while building internal sense of power and authority that supports assertive communication without aggressive behaviors that might trigger defensive responses from other parties.

Implement clarity breathing that focuses on slow, deliberate inhalation to enhance mental focus while providing optimal oxygenation for peak brain function during complex negotiations that require creative problem-solving and strategic thinking under pressure.

Begin each practice with four counts of inhalation through the nose while visualizing confidence and determination filling your body with the strength necessary to advocate effectively for your legitimate interests and needs without compromise or apology.

Visualization for Successful Outcomes

Success visualization that imagines positive outcomes while feeling the emotional satisfaction of favorable agreement builds confidence while programming your subconscious mind to recognize and pursue opportunities that lead to desired results through strategic action and persistent advocacy.

Process visualization that mentally rehearses negotiation conversations builds familiarity with likely scenarios while preparing responses to common objections and developing comfort with negotiation dynamics that might otherwise feel intimidating or overwhelming to inexperienced negotiators.

Relationship visualization that sees negotiation as collaboration rather than conflict creates positive expectations while building empathy for other parties' perspectives and constraints that must be accommodated in successful agreements that serve everyone's legitimate interests.

Practice outcome imagery by seeing yourself receiving favorable terms while feeling the satisfaction and relief that comes from successful advocacy that improves your financial situation while demonstrating your ability to create positive change through strategic communication and persistent effort.

Affirmations for Negotiation Power

Identity affirmations that reinforce your right to advocate for favorable terms build the self-concept necessary for confident negotiation while overcoming internal messages that might suggest you should accept whatever terms are initially offered without exploration of alternatives.

Worth affirmations that acknowledge your value in every transaction create the internal foundation for requesting appropriate compensation while recognizing that fair exchange requires advocacy from both parties and that mutual benefit serves everyone's interests most effectively.

Abundance affirmations that focus on mutual benefit and creative solutions prevent scarcity thinking that might lead to aggressive tactics or premature concessions through fear of losing opportunities that might not actually exist or might return through patient persistence.

Integrate daily affirmations such as "I don't just ask—I claim what serves my highest good while creating value for others" to reinforce your right to advocate for favorable terms while maintaining focus on collaborative solutions that benefit all parties involved.

Your Negotiation Transformation Journey

Developing negotiation mastery requires systematic practice that begins with low-stakes opportunities while building skills and confidence that enable successful advocacy in high-impact situations affecting your long-term financial well-being and professional success.

Start by identifying three current expenses where improved terms could provide immediate financial benefits through respectful but persistent advocacy. Practice tactical silence in everyday conversations while building comfort with pauses that create space for strategic thinking rather than immediate responses.

Research negotiation opportunities in your regular expenses while understanding that every interaction represents a chance to build skills that compound over time into significant financial benefits and improved relationships that support your ongoing prosperity and personal satisfaction.

Remember that negotiation excellence develops through consistent practice rather than perfect performance, making every interaction an opportunity to refine techniques that serve your highest good while honoring the legitimate interests of others with whom you engage in value exchange.

Foundation Building

Begin with subscription services and recurring expenses where relationship damage carries minimal risk, but success provides immediate confidence building and financial benefits. These low-stakes environments allow skill development without jeopardizing important relationships or significant opportunities.

Practice information gathering through open-ended questions in service situations while developing comfort with exploring alternatives that might not be immediately obvious but could provide superior value or improved terms that better serve your specific needs and circumstances.

Implement strategic silence when offered initial terms while observing how pauses create additional information and potential concessions that demonstrate the power of patient advocacy and thoughtful consideration in creating favorable outcomes for all parties involved.

Advanced Application

Apply learned techniques to more significant negotiations involving housing, employment, and financial services while building expertise in conversations that can dramatically impact your lifetime financial trajectory and professional development opportunities.

Develop timing awareness by identifying optimal windows for various types of requests while leveraging seasonal factors, business cycles, and organizational pressures that create motivation for favorable terms and creative problem-solving that serves mutual interests.

Build evidence collection systems that document your value as customer, employee, or service provider while creating objective basis for requests that demonstrate mutual benefit rather than one-sided demands that might create adversarial dynamics or relationship damage.

Final Takeaway

Negotiation isn't confrontation—it's calibration. You're not demanding more. You're demanding fair. And when you do it with clarity, calm, and conviction, you don't just win deals—you build a life that respects your value.

This profound truth transforms every conversation from potential conflict into opportunity for mutual elevation. When you approach negotiation as calibration rather than combat, you create space for solutions that serve everyone while ensuring that your worth receives appropriate recognition and compensation.

Your clarity about value, combined with calm persistence and unwavering conviction in your right to fair treatment, creates the foundation for negotiations that strengthen rather than strain relationships while achieving outcomes that honor your legitimate interests and aspirations.

Through this practice, you build not just better deals, but a better life—one where your value is recognized, your contributions are appropriately compensated, and your voice is heard with respect and consideration in every exchange that affects your prosperity and well-being.

The conversation that changes everything begins with your next negotiation. Approach it with the wisdom, confidence, and grace that transforms ordinary interactions into extraordinary opportunities for mutual benefit and personal empowerment.

Remember: you deserve fair value for everything you offer to the world, and negotiation is simply the respectful art of ensuring that this fairness becomes reality in every aspect of your life. Step forward with confidence, speak your worth with clarity, and watch as the world rises to meet your elevated expectations.

Chapter 6: Debt—The Devil and the Deal

"Debt is not inherently evil, nor is it inherently good. It is a powerful force that amplifies your financial choices—magnifying both wisdom and folly. The key to mastering debt lies not in avoiding it entirely, but in understanding its nature and wielding it with the precision of a master craftsman."

This is one of the most consequential chapters in your financial awakening, where we embark together on a journey to demystify one of the most misunderstood forces in the realm of wealth building. Here, within these pages, you will discover that debt occupies a paradoxical space in our financial lives—simultaneously capable of serving as the foundation for extraordinary prosperity and the architect of profound financial ruin.

As we venture into this exploration, I invite you to release any preconceived notions you may hold about debt being uniformly destructive or universally beneficial. Instead, let us approach this topic with the curiosity of explorers charting new territory, recognizing that the same force that has destroyed countless financial futures has also been the catalyst for some of history's greatest wealth creation stories.

The wisdom contained within this chapter will transform your relationship with debt from one of fear or reckless abandon to one of strategic understanding and purposeful application. Together, we will uncover the secrets that separate those who are enslaved by debt from those who harness its power to accelerate their journey toward financial freedom.

The Dual Nature of Financial Leverage

In the grand theater of personal finance, debt plays a starring role that is neither villain nor hero, but rather a complex character whose impact depends entirely upon how skillfully it is directed. This fundamental understanding forms the cornerstone of financial wisdom—recognizing that debt itself is merely a tool, and like any powerful tool, its value lies not in its existence but in the skill and intention with which it is wielded.

The conventional narrative surrounding debt often paints it with broad strokes, declaring it either categorically dangerous or universally beneficial. Yet this oversimplification fails to capture the nuanced reality that debt exists on a spectrum of usefulness, with some forms serving as stepping stones to prosperity while others function as quicksand that pulls borrowers deeper into financial distress.

Consider the profound difference between borrowing money to purchase a home that will appreciate in value and provide shelter for decades, versus borrowing money to fund a luxury vacation that provides temporary pleasure but no lasting value. Both involve debt, both require repayment with interest, yet their impact on your financial future could not be more different.

This distinction reveals the first principle of debt mastery: the purpose behind the borrowing determines whether debt becomes a catalyst for wealth creation or an impediment to financial progress.

When debt is employed strategically to acquire assets that generate income or appreciate in value, it transforms from a burden into a bridge—connecting your current financial position to your future prosperity.

Understanding the Leverage Equation

The concept of leverage in finance mirrors its application in physics—using a tool to amplify force and achieve results that would be impossible through direct effort alone. Financial leverage allows you to control assets and opportunities that exceed your immediate financial capacity, potentially multiplying your returns while also magnifying your risks.

When you purchase a home with a mortgage, you are employing leverage to control an asset worth hundreds of thousands of dollars with a down payment representing only a fraction of that value. If the home appreciates in value, your returns are calculated based on the full value of the property, not merely your initial investment. This amplification effect can dramatically accelerate wealth building when applied wisely.

However, leverage cuts both ways with mathematical precision. Just as it can amplify gains, it can equally amplify losses. The same mortgage that accelerates your wealth during a real estate boom can become a financial anchor during a market downturn, demonstrating why understanding leverage requires both optimism about potential gains and respect for possible risks.

Good Debt vs. Bad Debt: The Fundamental Distinction

The classification of debt into "good" and "bad" categories provides a practical framework for evaluating borrowing decisions, yet this distinction requires deeper exploration to be truly useful in your wealth-building journey. The difference lies not merely in the interest rate or repayment terms, but in the fundamental question: does this debt increase your net worth over time or diminish it?

Good Debt: The Wealth Builder's Ally

Good debt possesses characteristics that align with long-term wealth creation, serving as a strategic tool for acquiring assets or capabilities that generate value exceeding the cost of borrowing. These forms of debt share several common attributes that distinguish them from their destructive counterparts.

Mortgage Debt: The Foundation of Wealth Building

For most individuals, a home mortgage represents their introduction to good debt, providing access to real estate ownership that would otherwise require decades of saving. The strategic value of mortgage debt extends beyond mere homeownership, encompassing tax advantages, inflation hedging, and the powerful wealth-building force of leverage.

When you secure a mortgage to purchase a primary residence, you create multiple wealth-building dynamics simultaneously. The forced savings aspect of mortgage payments builds equity over time, while potential appreciation increases the underlying asset value. Additionally, the tax deductibility of mortgage interest in many jurisdictions effectively reduces the true cost of borrowing, making this form of debt even more attractive from a wealth-building perspective.

Consider Sarah, a young professional who chose to purchase a modest home rather than continue renting. Her $300,000 home purchase with a 20% down payment created immediate benefits: her monthly housing costs remained similar to rent, but now built equity rather than providing pure expense. Over fifteen years, her disciplined payments combined with modest appreciation resulted in $180,000 in home equity, representing wealth that would not have existed through renting.

Investment Property Financing: Scaling Real Estate Success

The principles of good debt extend beyond primary residence mortgages to encompass investment property financing, where borrowed funds acquire assets specifically intended to generate income and appreciate in value. This application of leverage can exponentially accelerate wealth building for those who master its intricacies.

Investment property financing transforms individual investors into real estate entrepreneurs, enabling them to control multiple income-producing assets without requiring the full purchase price in cash. The rental income from these properties ideally covers the mortgage payments, taxes, and maintenance costs while providing positive cash flow and long-term appreciation benefits.

David's real estate journey illustrates this concept perfectly. Starting with a single rental property purchased with 25% down, he used the positive cash flow and appreciation to qualify for additional investment properties. Over ten years, he assembled a portfolio of six rental properties with a combined value of $1.8 million, using only $180,000 of his own money as down payments. The remaining $1.62 million in value was controlled through strategic use of good debt.

Education Debt: Investing in Human Capital

Student loans occupy a unique position in the debt spectrum, representing investment in human capital that can generate returns for an entire career. However, not all educational debt qualifies as good debt—the key lies in ensuring that the education acquired generates sufficient additional income to justify the borrowing costs.

Strategic educational borrowing focuses on degrees and certifications that demonstrably increase earning potential, particularly in fields with strong employment prospects and salary growth trajectories. The calculation involves comparing the total cost of education (including opportunity costs) against the lifetime increase in earning potential attributable to the degree.

Maria's nursing degree exemplifies strategic educational debt utilization. Her $35,000 in student loans enabled her to transition from retail work earning $25,000 annually to a nursing career starting at $55,000 with clear advancement opportunities. The additional $30,000 in annual income more than justified the educational investment, with the degree paying for itself within two years while providing decades of enhanced earning potential.

Business Debt: Funding Entrepreneurial Ventures

Business loans and lines of credit can represent excellent debt when used to fund ventures with clear paths to profitability and growth. This category includes equipment financing, inventory loans, and working capital lines of credit that enable businesses to operate and expand more efficiently than would be possible with cash-only operations.

The key to successful business debt lies in ensuring that borrowed funds generate returns exceeding their costs. Equipment financing that enables increased production capacity, inventory loans that prevent stockouts during peak demand periods, and working capital lines that smooth cash flow fluctuations all represent strategic uses of business debt.

Bad Debt: The Wealth Destroyer

Bad debt possesses characteristics that diminish net worth over time, typically financing consumption rather than investment and carrying high interest rates that compound financial stress rather than creating wealth. Understanding these destructive forms of debt empowers you to avoid the traps that keep millions locked in cycles of financial struggle.

Credit Card Debt: The Modern Financial Quicksand

Credit card debt represents perhaps the most pervasive form of bad debt in modern society, seducing consumers with convenience while charging interest rates that make wealth building nearly impossible. The average credit card interest rate exceeds 20% annually, creating a mathematical barrier to financial progress that few can overcome while carrying significant balances.

The insidious nature of credit card debt lies in its design to encourage minimum payments that barely cover interest charges, extending repayment periods indefinitely while maximizing profit for lenders. A $5,000 credit card balance with an 18% interest rate, paid with minimum payments of $100 monthly, would require over 30 years to pay off while generating more than $8,000 in interest payments.

Consider the opportunity cost of credit card debt: money spent on interest payments cannot be invested for wealth building. The same $200 monthly payment used to service credit card debt could instead be invested to generate substantial long-term wealth through compound interest and market appreciation.

Auto Loans: The Depreciating Asset Trap

Vehicle loans occupy a gray area in debt classification, potentially serving transportation needs while simultaneously destroying wealth through the financing of rapidly depreciating assets. The challenge lies in distinguishing between necessary transportation financing and lifestyle inflation disguised as practical necessity.

The average new car loses approximately 20% of its value in the first year and 60% within five years, making auto loans a form of debt that finances declining asset values. When combined with extended loan terms that can exceed the vehicle's useful life, auto financing often creates situations where borrowers owe more than their vehicles are worth.

Strategic vehicle financing focuses on reliable, fuel-efficient transportation rather than lifestyle statements. Purchasing certified pre-owned vehicles with shorter loan terms minimizes the wealth destruction inherent in vehicle financing while still meeting legitimate transportation needs.

Lifestyle Debt: The Prosperity Killer

The most destructive category of debt encompasses borrowing for lifestyle enhancement rather than wealth building—vacations, luxury goods, entertainment, and consumption that provides temporary satisfaction but no lasting value. This debt category includes personal loans for non-investment purposes, store financing for furniture and electronics, and any borrowing that funds experiences or possessions without generating returns.

The mathematical reality of lifestyle debt is stark: every dollar borrowed for consumption must be repaid with interest from future income, reducing your capacity for saving and investing while providing no offsetting asset or income enhancement. This creates a vicious cycle where lifestyle debt undermines the very financial progress needed to achieve the lifestyle originally desired.

Interest Mechanics: The Mathematics of Money

Understanding how interest works—both in your favor and against you—provides the foundation for making informed debt decisions and maximizing the wealth-building potential of strategic borrowing. The mechanics of interest represent one of the most powerful forces in finance, capable of creating extraordinary wealth or devastating financial destruction depending upon which side of the equation you occupy.

Compound Interest: Your Greatest Enemy or Ally

The power of compound interest that works magnificently in investment accounts becomes your greatest financial enemy when applied to debt balances. Credit card companies and other lenders harness this same mathematical principle to extract maximum profit from borrowers, turning modest balances into substantial long-term obligations through the relentless accumulation of interest charges.

When you carry debt balances, you are essentially paying compound interest in reverse—your debt grows exponentially if not managed properly, while your wealth-building capacity diminishes accordingly. A credit card balance that seems manageable at first can spiral into unmanageable proportions when minimum payments fail to keep pace with compound interest accumulation.

Conversely, when you position yourself as a lender through investments, compound interest becomes your powerful ally, growing your wealth exponentially over time. The same mathematical principle that makes debt dangerous makes investing profitable, highlighting the critical importance of being on the correct side of the interest equation.

The True Cost of Borrowing

The sticker price of debt—the stated interest rate—often understates the true cost of borrowing when additional fees, extended terms, and opportunity costs are considered. Developing the ability to calculate real borrowing costs empowers you to make informed decisions about when debt makes financial sense and when it represents wealth destruction.

Consider a typical payday loan advertised at a seemingly modest fee of $15 per $100 borrowed for two weeks. This arrangement translates to an annual percentage rate exceeding 390%, making it one of the most expensive forms of borrowing available. Yet the marketing focuses on the dollar amount rather than the true annual cost, demonstrating how inadequate cost analysis can lead to devastating financial decisions.

Similarly, extended warranty financing, rent-to-own arrangements, and other consumer financing options often carry hidden costs that dramatically exceed their stated terms. The ability to calculate true annual percentage rates and compare them to alternative financing options protects you from predatory lending practices while highlighting superior alternatives.

Leverage Strategies: Amplifying Success

When employed strategically, leverage can dramatically accelerate wealth building by allowing you to control assets and opportunities exceeding your immediate financial capacity. However, successful leverage requires careful attention to risk management, cash flow analysis, and market conditions that could affect your ability to service debt obligations.

Real Estate Leverage Optimization

Real estate investment provides one of the most accessible applications of wealth-building leverage, enabling individuals to control valuable assets with modest down payments while benefiting from rental income, tax advantages, and long-term appreciation. The key to successful real estate leverage lies in ensuring that rental income exceeds all carrying costs while maintaining adequate reserves for maintenance and vacancy periods.

Conservative real estate investors typically target properties where rental income exceeds mortgage payments, taxes, insurance, and estimated maintenance costs by at least 10%. This margin provides protection against market fluctuations while generating positive cash flow that can be reinvested for additional property acquisitions.

Business Leverage Applications

Business owners can employ leverage to fund growth opportunities that generate returns exceeding borrowing costs, whether through equipment purchases that increase productivity, inventory investments that prevent sales losses, or working capital that enables larger contract acceptance.

The analysis involves comparing the cost of borrowed funds against the additional profits generated by the leverage. Equipment financing at 8% annual interest makes financial sense when the equipment generates productivity improvements worth 15% annually, creating a net positive return of 7% on the leverage employed.

Emotional Traps and Psychological Debt Patterns

The relationship between psychology and debt extends far beyond mathematical calculations, encompassing emotional patterns, behavioral tendencies, and subconscious beliefs that can sabotage even the most well-intentioned debt management strategies. Understanding these psychological dynamics empowers you to recognize and overcome the emotional traps that keep millions trapped in cycles of destructive borrowing.

The Psychology of Instant Gratification

Modern consumer culture deliberately exploits psychological weaknesses related to instant gratification, creating powerful emotional impulses to borrow money for immediate satisfaction rather than delayed gratification through patient saving. This exploitation represents one of the most significant obstacles to building long-term wealth, as it undermines the very patience and discipline required for compound interest to work its magic.

The neurological basis for instant gratification preferences lies in primitive brain structures that evolved to prioritize immediate survival needs over long-term planning. In prehistoric environments, this preference served important survival functions, but in modern financial contexts, it becomes a liability that undermines wealth-building efforts.

Credit card companies and other lenders deliberately design their products and marketing to trigger instant gratification responses, offering immediate purchasing power in exchange for future payments that seem abstract and distant. The psychological distance between present pleasure and future payment creates an illusion that minimizes the perceived cost of borrowing.

Overcoming Instant Gratification Through Systems

The antidote to instant gratification lies not in willpower alone, but in creating systems that make long-term thinking easier and more rewarding than impulsive decision-making. These systems include waiting periods before major purchases, automatic transfers to savings accounts, and reward structures that celebrate delayed gratification achievements.

The 24-hour rule for non-essential purchases over $100 provides a simple system for overcoming impulse buying. By creating a mandatory delay between desire and purchase, you allow rational thinking to override emotional impulses while often discovering that the initial urgency diminishes significantly with time.

Similarly, implementing automatic transfers to dedicated savings accounts for major purchases transforms the psychological dynamic from borrowing for instant gratification to saving for planned acquisition. This shift enhances the satisfaction derived from purchases while eliminating the stress and cost associated with debt financing.

Social Pressure and Lifestyle Inflation

Social comparison represents another powerful psychological force that drives destructive debt accumulation, as individuals attempt to maintain lifestyle appearances that exceed their current financial capacity. Social media exacerbates this tendency by providing constant exposure to carefully curated lifestyle presentations that create unrealistic expectations about normal spending patterns.

The psychological mechanism known as "lifestyle inflation" describes the tendency for spending to increase proportionally with income, preventing wealth accumulation despite rising earnings. This pattern often involves debt financing to bridge the gap between desired lifestyle and current financial capacity, creating an expensive cycle that undermines long-term financial security.

Building Immunity to Social Financial Pressure

Developing resistance to social financial pressure requires clear personal values, strong financial goals, and supportive social networks that prioritize financial health over lifestyle appearances. This process involves both internal work to clarify your authentic priorities and external work to build relationships with financially responsible individuals.

Creating a personal mission statement that clearly articulates your financial priorities provides a foundation for resisting social pressure to overspend. When faced with pressure to participate in expensive social activities or purchase status symbols, you can reference your mission statement to maintain focus on long-term wealth building rather than short-term social approval.

Building relationships with financially responsible individuals creates positive peer pressure that supports wealth-building behaviors rather than undermining them. Seek out friends, mentors, and social groups that celebrate financial discipline, strategic thinking, and long-term planning rather than conspicuous consumption and lifestyle inflation.

Debt Shame and Financial Avoidance

Many individuals struggling with debt experience shame, embarrassment, and anxiety that leads to financial avoidance behaviors—refusing to examine their debt situation honestly, avoiding debt payment responsibilities, and postponing necessary financial decisions. These avoidance patterns typically worsen debt problems while creating additional stress and anxiety.

The shame associated with debt problems often stems from societal messages that equate financial struggles with personal failure, despite the reality that many debt problems result from circumstances beyond individual control, such as medical emergencies, job loss, or economic downturns. This shame becomes counterproductive when it prevents individuals from taking constructive action to address their debt situations.

Transforming Shame into Empowerment

The path from debt shame to financial empowerment involves reframing debt problems as temporary challenges that can be overcome through education, planning, and consistent action rather than permanent personal failures that define your worth or capability.

Begin by acknowledging that debt problems are extremely common and that many successful individuals have overcome significant financial challenges through strategic thinking and persistent effort. This perspective shift reduces the shame associated with debt while increasing confidence in your ability to create positive change.

Focus on progress rather than perfection by celebrating small wins along your debt elimination journey. Each payment made, each unnecessary expense avoided, and each positive financial decision represents meaningful progress toward your goals, regardless of how much work remains to be done.

Debt Detox: Cleansing Your Financial System

Just as physical detoxification eliminates harmful substances from your body, financial debt detox removes the accumulated financial toxins that impair your wealth-building capacity while establishing healthy financial habits that support long-term prosperity. This process requires both immediate interventions to address current debt problems and systematic changes to prevent future debt accumulation.

Emergency Financial Triage

When debt balances have reached crisis levels, emergency triage becomes necessary to prevent further deterioration while creating breathing room for longer-term debt elimination strategies. This process involves rapidly identifying the most dangerous debt situations while implementing immediate protective measures.

High-Interest Debt Prioritization

Begin your debt detox by creating a comprehensive inventory of all outstanding debts, including balances, interest rates, minimum payments, and payment due dates. This inventory provides the foundation for strategic debt elimination planning while ensuring that no obligations are overlooked during the detox process.

Prioritize high-interest debt for immediate attention, as these balances create the greatest drain on your financial resources while offering the largest potential savings through elimination. Credit card balances, payday loans, and other high-cost debt should receive maximum payment allocation while minimum payments are made on lower-cost obligations.

The mathematical principle behind this prioritization strategy, known as the debt avalanche method, minimizes the total interest paid during debt elimination while maximizing the speed of balance reduction. By focusing extra payments on the highest-interest debt first, you reduce the overall cost of debt elimination while building momentum through rapid balance reductions.

Cash Flow Stabilization

Emergency debt detox also requires immediate cash flow stabilization to prevent additional borrowing while creating capacity for debt elimination payments. This process involves both expense reduction and income enhancement strategies implemented simultaneously for maximum impact.

Expense reduction during debt detox focuses on eliminating non-essential spending while maintaining necessary living expenses and debt service obligations. This might involve temporary lifestyle adjustments such as cooking at home instead of dining out, canceling subscription services, and postponing discretionary purchases until debt balances are eliminated.

Income enhancement opportunities during debt detox might include selling unused possessions, accepting additional work hours, pursuing freelance opportunities, or monetizing skills and hobbies. The goal is creating immediate cash flow improvement that can be directed toward debt elimination while establishing income diversification habits that support long-term financial stability.

The Debt Elimination Blueprint

Systematic debt elimination requires a structured approach that maintains motivation through visible progress while optimizing the mathematical efficiency of debt reduction. The most effective debt elimination strategies combine psychological motivation with mathematical optimization to create sustainable progress toward debt freedom.

The Snowball vs. Avalanche Method Debate

Two primary strategies dominate debt elimination discussions: the debt snowball method, which prioritizes smallest balances first to create psychological momentum, and the debt avalanche method, which prioritizes highest interest rates to minimize total interest paid. Both approaches have merit, and the optimal choice depends on your psychological makeup and debt composition.

The debt snowball method proves particularly effective for individuals who need psychological motivation to maintain their debt elimination efforts. By eliminating smaller balances first, you create a series of early victories that build confidence and momentum for tackling larger debts. This approach sacrifices some mathematical efficiency in favor of psychological sustainability.

The debt avalanche method maximizes mathematical efficiency by minimizing total interest payments, making it ideal for individuals who are motivated by logical optimization rather than psychological reinforcement. This approach typically results in faster debt elimination and lower total costs, particularly when high-interest balances are substantial.

Hybrid Elimination Strategies

Many successful debt eliminators employ hybrid strategies that combine elements of both approaches, such as beginning with the snowball method to build momentum before switching to the avalanche method for larger balances. This approach provides both psychological motivation and mathematical optimization while adapting to changing circumstances during the elimination process.

Another effective hybrid approach involves targeting the highest-interest debt that can be eliminated within six months, providing both psychological victory and meaningful interest savings. This strategy ensures regular progress celebrations while maintaining focus on mathematical efficiency.

Creating Debt-Prevention Systems

The ultimate goal of debt detox extends beyond eliminating current balances to creating systems that prevent future debt accumulation while supporting sustainable wealth building. These prevention systems address both the practical aspects of financial management and the psychological patterns that contribute to debt problems.

Emergency Fund Development

Building an emergency fund represents the most critical debt prevention strategy, providing financial cushioning for unexpected expenses that might otherwise require borrowing. The traditional recommendation of three to six months of expenses in emergency savings provides substantial protection against most financial emergencies while eliminating the need for credit card usage during crises.

Start emergency fund development even while eliminating debt by directing small amounts to a separate savings account dedicated to emergency purposes. Even $500 in emergency savings can prevent minor financial setbacks from derailing your debt elimination efforts while building the habit of automatic savings that will serve you throughout your wealth-building journey.

As debt balances decrease, gradually increase emergency fund contributions until you reach your target balance. This parallel approach ensures that debt elimination doesn't leave you vulnerable to future financial shocks while establishing the savings habits essential for long-term financial stability.

Spending Automation and Controls

Automated financial systems remove the daily decision-making burden that can lead to poor spending choices while ensuring that essential financial goals receive priority over discretionary spending. These systems include automatic bill payments, savings transfers, and investment contributions that occur without requiring ongoing willpower or memory.

Implement spending controls that make impulsive purchases more difficult while providing cooling-off periods for major financial decisions. This might involve removing stored payment information from online retailers, implementing waiting periods for non-essential purchases, or requiring spousal approval for expenditures above predetermined thresholds.

Create visual reminders of your financial goals and progress that reinforce positive financial behaviors while discouraging counterproductive spending. This might include debt elimination charts, savings goal trackers, or visual representations of your long-term financial objectives prominently displayed in your living space.

Your Debt Mastery Action Plan

Transforming your relationship with debt from one of confusion or fear to one of strategic mastery requires systematic implementation of the principles and strategies outlined in this chapter. Your journey toward debt mastery begins with honest assessment of your current situation and progresses through strategic planning, consistent implementation, and continuous refinement of your approach.

Phase 1: Debt Assessment and Strategy Selection (Week 1)

Complete Debt Inventory Creation

Document every debt obligation you currently carry, including credit cards, student loans, auto loans, mortgages, personal loans, and any informal borrowing arrangements. For each debt, record the current balance, minimum payment, interest rate, and payment due date. This comprehensive inventory provides the foundation for all subsequent debt management decisions.

Calculate the total amount you pay monthly in debt service and the percentage of your income dedicated to debt payments. This analysis reveals the magnitude of your debt burden while highlighting the cash flow that will become available for wealth building as debts are eliminated.

Strategy Selection Based on Personal Psychology

Choose between snowball and avalanche debt elimination methods based on your psychological makeup and motivation patterns. If you need regular victories to maintain motivation, select the snowball method. If you are primarily motivated by mathematical optimization, choose the avalanche method.

Consider hybrid approaches if your debt composition suggests benefits from combining strategies. The key is selecting an approach you can implement consistently rather than the theoretically optimal method you might abandon due to motivational challenges.

Phase 2: Emergency Interventions and Cash Flow Optimization (Week 2)

Immediate Expense Reduction Implementation

Identify and eliminate non-essential expenses that can be redirected toward debt elimination without significantly impacting your quality of life. Focus on subscription services, dining out, entertainment expenses, and discretionary purchases that can be temporarily suspended during your debt elimination period.

Calculate the monthly amount freed through expense reductions and commit this amount to accelerated debt elimination payments. This calculation demonstrates the direct impact of lifestyle adjustments on your debt elimination timeline while providing motivation for maintaining expense discipline.

Income Enhancement Exploration

Identify immediate opportunities for increasing income through overtime work, freelance projects, selling unused possessions, or monetizing existing skills and hobbies. The goal is creating additional cash flow specifically dedicated to debt elimination rather than lifestyle enhancement.

Commit any additional income generated during your debt elimination period exclusively to debt payments rather than lifestyle improvements. This discipline accelerates your progress while establishing habits that will support wealth building once debt elimination is complete.

Phase 3: System Implementation and Progress Tracking (Weeks 3-4)

Automated Payment System Setup

Establish automatic payments for all debt obligations to ensure consistent payment timing while avoiding late fees that can derail your elimination efforts. Set automatic payments for amounts exceeding minimum requirements based on your selected elimination strategy.

Create automatic transfers from your checking account to a dedicated debt elimination savings account if needed to accumulate funds for large payments or to smooth irregular income patterns. This system ensures consistent progress regardless of income timing variations.

Progress Monitoring and Motivation Systems

Develop visual tracking systems that make your debt elimination progress visible and rewarding. This might include debt thermometers, balance reduction charts, or applications that gamify the debt elimination process through achievement recognition and milestone celebrations.

Schedule regular progress reviews to assess the effectiveness of your debt elimination strategy while making necessary adjustments based on changing circumstances. These reviews maintain accountability while ensuring your approach remains optimized for your current situation.

Phase 4: Long-Term Debt Prevention and Wealth Building Transition (Ongoing)

Emergency Fund Development

Begin building emergency fund reserves even while eliminating debt by directing small amounts to separate savings accounts dedicated to emergency purposes. This parallel approach provides protection against setbacks while establishing essential savings habits.

Gradually increase emergency fund contributions as debt balances decrease, with the goal of fully funding your emergency reserves immediately upon debt elimination completion. This transition ensures seamless movement from debt elimination to wealth building without vulnerable periods.

Wealth Building System Preparation

Research and prepare investment accounts and wealth building systems that can be activated immediately upon debt elimination completion. This preparation ensures that the cash flow freed through debt elimination transitions immediately to wealth building rather than lifestyle inflation.

Educate yourself about investment strategies, account types, and wealth building approaches while completing debt elimination so that you can implement sophisticated wealth building strategies immediately upon achieving debt freedom.

The Liberation That Awaits

As we conclude this exploration of debt's dual nature, remember that you now possess the knowledge and tools necessary to transform debt from a source of financial stress into a strategic wealth-building instrument. The principles you have learned apply regardless of your current debt situation, providing both immediate relief for debt problems and long-term strategies for leveraging debt to accelerate prosperity.

Your relationship with debt need no longer be characterized by fear, confusion, or avoidance. Instead, you can approach debt decisions with confidence, armed with clear criteria for distinguishing beneficial borrowing from wealth destruction and equipped with systematic strategies for eliminating harmful debt while strategically employing beneficial leverage.

The journey from debt slave to debt master requires patience, discipline, and consistent application of the principles outlined in this chapter. Yet this transformation represents one of the most powerful steps you can take toward financial freedom, as mastering debt provides both immediate cash flow relief and long-term wealth building acceleration.

Chapter Challenge: Begin Your Debt Transformation

This Week:

- Complete a comprehensive debt inventory including all balances, rates, and payments
- Calculate your total monthly debt service and debt-to-income ratio
- Choose your debt elimination strategy based on your psychological preferences
- Identify $100 in monthly expenses that can be redirected to debt elimination

This Month:

- Implement your chosen debt elimination strategy with automated payments
- Create visual tracking systems to monitor your progress and maintain motivation
- Begin emergency fund development even if starting with only $25 monthly
- Research and prepare wealth building strategies for post-debt elimination implementation

This Quarter:

- Achieve your first debt elimination victory, whether through snowball or avalanche methods
- Establish automated systems that prevent future debt accumulation
- Build emergency fund reserves to at least $1,000 to provide basic financial protection
- Educate yourself about strategic debt usage for future wealth building opportunities

Remember that debt mastery is not about avoiding all debt forever, but about understanding when debt serves your wealth-building goals and when it undermines them. The same mathematical forces that make debt dangerous when used poorly become powerful wealth-building tools when employed strategically.

Your wealth rebellion continues with every debt payment that frees future cash flow for investment, every strategic borrowing decision that accelerates asset acquisition, and every debt elimination victory that moves you closer to financial independence. The chains of destructive debt are breaking, revealing the pathways to prosperity that have always existed beneath the surface.

In our next chapter, we will explore the legal frameworks that protect consumers from predatory lending practices while empowering you to exercise your rights when dealing with creditors and collection agencies. Because understanding debt is powerful, but knowing your legal protections makes you truly formidable in the financial arena.

The devil and the deal await your decision. Choose wisely, and transform debt from your master into your servant in the grand pursuit of financial freedom and lasting wealth.

Chapter 7: Applying Law to Credit Debt

"The law is not merely a shield to protect the innocent—it is a sword to cut through the chains of financial bondage. In your hands, legal knowledge becomes the key that unlocks doors once thought permanently sealed, transforming your relationship with debt from one of helpless servitude to strategic mastery."

This chapter will fundamentally alter your perspective on your connection with credit debt and the individuals who attempt to collect it. Within these pages, we set out on a voyage that goes beyond simple financial guidance, venturing into a territory where legal understanding becomes your strongest tool against exploitative tactics and unjust treatment.

As we venture together into this empowering territory, I invite you to embrace a fundamental shift in perspective. You are not merely a debtor at the mercy of creditors—you are a consumer protected by decades of hard-won legal victories, armed with rights that carry the full force of federal and state law. The strategies we will explore represent the culmination of countless battles fought by ordinary people who refused to accept that financial struggles meant surrendering their dignity or legal protections.

This chapter serves as your practical guide to wielding the legal protections we discussed previously, transforming theoretical knowledge into real-world power that can save you thousands of dollars while protecting your financial future. Together, we will explore the art and science of strategic debt management, where every letter you write, every conversation you have, and every decision you make is informed by deep understanding of your rights and the legal obligations of those who seek payment from you.

The Foundation of Legal Debt Strategy

In the complex ecosystem of credit and debt, knowledge of your legal rights serves as the cornerstone upon which all effective strategies are built. The laws that protect consumers were not created in ivory towers by abstract theorists, but forged in the crucible of real human experience—families destroyed by abusive collection practices, individuals crushed beneath the weight of illegal fees and charges, and countless Americans who discovered that their financial struggles were compounded by those who would exploit their vulnerability.

Every protection we will explore in this chapter exists because someone before you fought for it, challenged it in court, or worked tirelessly to ensure that future generations would possess tools for fighting back against financial predators. This historical context is not merely academic—it reminds us that the rights you possess today were hard-won victories that deserve both respect and active utilization.

The strategic application of these legal protections requires understanding that debt collection has become an industry unto itself, with its own rules, procedures, and profit motives that often conflict with consumer interests. Original creditors frequently sell debts to collection agencies for pennies on the dollar, creating an entire ecosystem of businesses whose success depends upon collecting money from consumers who may not fully understand their rights or the legal limitations on collection activities.

Understanding the Debt Collection Ecosystem

The moment your account becomes delinquent with an original creditor, you enter a complex world populated by specialized businesses whose primary expertise lies in extracting money from reluctant consumers. This ecosystem includes collection departments within original creditor companies, third-party collection agencies that work on commission, debt buyers who purchase portfolios of delinquent accounts, and law firms that specialize in debt collection litigation.

Each participant in this ecosystem operates under different legal constraints and possesses different levels of motivation to pursue collection activities. Original creditors, having already received tax write-offs for uncollectible debts, may be more willing to negotiate reasonable settlements. Third-party collectors working on commission may employ more aggressive tactics to maximize their returns. Debt buyers, having purchased accounts for small fractions of their face value, can afford to be extremely persistent while still generating profits from modest collection percentages.

Understanding these different motivations and constraints empowers you to tailor your strategies appropriately for each situation. The letter that works effectively with an original creditor may require modification when dealing with a debt buyer, while the negotiation approach that succeeds with a collection agency might fail entirely when applied to a law firm pursuing litigation.

The Psychology of Power Dynamics

Debt collection activities often involve deliberate attempts to create psychological pressure that encourages immediate payment without careful consideration of your rights or options. Collection agents receive training in techniques designed to create urgency, fear, and emotional responses that override rational decision-making. They may claim that settlement offers are only available for limited periods, suggest that legal consequences are imminent, or imply that cooperation is your only option for avoiding more serious problems.

Recognizing these psychological tactics empowers you to maintain emotional equilibrium while making rational decisions based on facts rather than manufactured urgency. The most effective debt management strategies require clear thinking unclouded by emotional manipulation, enabling you to evaluate offers objectively while pursuing outcomes that serve your long-term financial interests.

Your understanding of legal protections serves as an antidote to these psychological pressure tactics, providing objective frameworks for evaluating collection attempts and making informed decisions about how to respond. When you know your rights, collection agents lose their ability to pressure you through misinformation or intimidation, fundamentally altering the power dynamics of debt collection interactions.

Dispute Procedures: Your First Line of Defense

The dispute process represents your most fundamental protection against erroneous, inflated, or entirely invalid debt collection attempts. This process, rooted in federal consumer protection laws, places the burden of proof on debt collectors to verify that debts are legitimate, accurate, and legally collectible. Understanding how to effectively utilize dispute procedures can eliminate invalid debts entirely while potentially reducing legitimate debts to more manageable amounts.

The power of dispute procedures lies not merely in their ability to challenge incorrect information, but in their capacity to force debt collectors to produce documentation that many cannot provide. The debt collection industry often operates on volume rather than precision, purchasing and selling portfolios of accounts with minimal documentation. When forced to prove their claims through formal dispute procedures, many collectors discover that they lack the records necessary to validate their collection attempts.

The Art of Effective Debt Validation

Debt validation represents your statutory right under the Fair Debt Collection Practices Act to require that debt collectors prove the validity and accuracy of their collection attempts. This process must be initiated within thirty days of receiving the collector's initial written communication, creating a narrow window that requires prompt action but offers powerful protection when properly utilized.

An effective debt validation request goes beyond simply asking collectors to "validate the debt." Instead, it should request specific documentation that demonstrates the collector's legal right to collect the debt, the accuracy of the amount claimed, and the chain of custody if the debt has been sold or transferred. This comprehensive approach maximizes your chances of discovering weaknesses in the collector's position while ensuring that any debt they can validate is accurate and legally enforceable.

Essential Elements of Comprehensive Debt Validation Requests:

Your validation request should demand specific documentation that debt collectors often cannot provide, including the original signed credit application or agreement, complete payment history showing how the current balance was calculated, documentation proving the collector's ownership of the debt, and verification that the debt has not exceeded applicable statutes of limitations.

Additionally, request that the collector provide their license to collect debts in your state, proof that they have complied with all applicable notice requirements, and verification that any fees or charges added to the original debt are legally permissible under the original agreement and applicable law.

This comprehensive approach often reveals deficiencies that can be leveraged in negotiations or used to challenge the collection entirely.

Strategic Validation Request Template

The following template provides a foundation for comprehensive debt validation requests that maximize your protection while ensuring compliance with legal requirements. This template should be modified based on your specific circumstances and the particular collection attempt you are addressing.

[Date]

[Collector Name and Address]

Re: Account Number [Account Number]—Debt Validation Request

Dear Sir or Madam:

I am in receipt of your letter dated [Date] regarding the above-referenced account. This letter serves as my formal request for validation of this alleged debt pursuant to my rights under the Fair Debt Collection Practices Act, 15 U.S.C. § 1692g.

Please provide the following documentation to validate this debt:

1. **Original Agreement**: A copy of the original signed credit application or agreement that allegedly created this debt, including all terms and conditions that were in effect when the account was opened.

1. **Complete Payment History**: A detailed accounting showing all payments, charges, fees, and interest applied to this account from inception to the current claimed balance, including dates and amounts of each transaction.

1. **Chain of Custody Documentation**: Complete documentation showing the chain of ownership of this debt, including all assignments, sales, or transfers from the original creditor to your organization.

1. **Legal Standing**: Documentation proving your organization's legal right to collect this debt, including any collection agreements, purchase agreements, or assignments that grant you collection authority.

1. **Licensing Documentation**: Proof that your organization is properly licensed to collect debts in [Your State] and that this license was valid at the time you began collection activities.

1. **Statute of Limitations Compliance**: Verification that this debt has not exceeded the

applicable statute of limitations for collection in [Your State].

1. **Fee and Charge Justification**: Documentation justifying any fees, charges, or interest that have been added to the original debt amount, including verification that such additions are permissible under the original agreement and applicable law.

Please be advised that I dispute this debt in its entirety until you provide adequate validation as requested above. During the validation period, I expect that you will comply with all requirements of the Fair Debt Collection Practices Act, including cessation of collection activities until validation is provided.

I request that all future communications regarding this matter be in writing. Do not contact me by telephone or at my place of employment.

Sincerely,
[Your Signature]
[Your Printed Name]
[Your Address]
SENT VIA CERTIFIED MAIL, RETURN RECEIPT REQUESTED

Advanced Validation Strategies for Complex Situations

When dealing with particularly aggressive collectors or complex debt situations, advanced validation strategies can provide additional protection while uncovering more substantial weaknesses in collection attempts. These strategies build upon basic validation requests while addressing specific challenges that arise in sophisticated debt collection operations.

Medical Debt Validation Considerations

Medical debts often involve complex billing relationships between healthcare providers, insurance companies, and collection agencies that create numerous opportunities for errors and violations. When validating medical debts, specifically request documentation showing that insurance benefits were properly applied, that all available discounts or charity care programs were considered, and that the healthcare provider followed all applicable state laws regarding medical debt collection.

Request copies of all insurance submissions and explanations of benefits, documentation of any charity care applications or eligibility determinations, and proof that the healthcare provider complied with all state-specific requirements for medical debt collection, which often include mandatory waiting periods and specific notice requirements.

Credit Card Debt Validation Complexities

Credit card debts present unique validation challenges because these accounts often involve complex terms and conditions that change over time, making it difficult for collectors to prove the exact terms that governed the account when it became delinquent. Request complete terms and conditions that were in effect throughout the life of the account, documentation of any changes to interest rates or fees, and proof that all regulatory disclosures required by the Truth in Lending Act were provided.

Additionally, demand complete records of all promotional rates, balance transfer terms, and any modifications to the original credit agreement, as collectors often cannot provide comprehensive documentation of these complex credit relationships.

Negotiation Strategies: The Art of Strategic Settlement

Once you have established your legal position through proper validation requests or dispute procedures, negotiation becomes the primary tool for resolving debt situations in ways that serve your financial interests while satisfying collector objectives. Effective negotiation requires understanding both the mathematical realities of debt collection economics and the psychological dynamics that influence decision-making on both sides of the negotiation.

Successful debt negotiation begins with recognizing that collectors, regardless of their aggressive tactics, are ultimately businesses seeking profitable outcomes rather than punishment or retribution. This business focus creates opportunities for mutually beneficial agreements that resolve debts for less than their full claimed amounts while providing collectors with returns that exceed their costs and meet their profitability requirements.

Understanding Collection Economics

The economics of debt collection create natural negotiation leverage that informed consumers can exploit to secure favorable settlement agreements. Collection agencies typically work on commission structures that provide them with percentages of collected amounts rather than fixed fees, creating incentives for them to accept reasonable settlements rather than pursue costly and uncertain collection litigation.

Debt buyers who purchase portfolios of delinquent accounts often pay between five and fifteen cents per dollar of claimed debt value, meaning they can generate substantial profits even when settling accounts for small fractions of their face values. Understanding these economics empowers you to make settlement offers that appear attractive to collectors while still providing you with significant savings compared to paying full claimed amounts.

Timing Considerations in Debt Negotiations

The timing of settlement negotiations can significantly impact the terms you can secure, as collector motivations and constraints change based on various factors including the age of the debt, their internal collection targets, and regulatory pressure. Accounts approaching statutory limitation deadlines become less valuable to collectors, creating opportunities for more aggressive negotiation positions.

Similarly, collection agencies often face quarterly or annual performance targets that can make them more willing to accept lower settlement amounts during specific periods. Understanding these timing dynamics enables you to structure negotiation approaches for maximum effectiveness while avoiding periods when collectors may be less willing to compromise.

Strategic Settlement Negotiation Framework

Effective debt settlement negotiations require systematic approaches that maximize your leverage while minimizing your exposure to unfavorable outcomes. This framework provides structured methods for approaching settlement discussions that protect your interests while creating pathways to mutually acceptable agreements.

Initial Settlement Positioning

Begin settlement negotiations from positions of strength by demonstrating your knowledge of legal protections and your willingness to exercise your rights if reasonable agreements cannot be reached. Reference any weaknesses you discovered during the validation process while making it clear that you prefer negotiated resolution to prolonged legal disputes.

Your initial settlement offer should be significantly lower than your ultimate acceptable amount, providing room for the natural give-and-take that characterizes successful negotiations. However, ensure that your initial offer is not so low as to be insulting or to suggest that you are not negotiating in good faith.

Payment Term Structuring

The structure of settlement payments can be as important as the total settlement amount, particularly for consumers facing cash flow constraints. Many collectors prefer lump-sum payments that provide immediate returns and eliminate ongoing administrative costs, potentially making them willing to accept lower total amounts in exchange for immediate payment.

However, if lump-sum payments are not feasible, structure payment plans that work within your budget while providing collectors with reasonable assurance of payment completion. Consider offering slightly higher total settlement amounts in exchange for extended payment terms, as this trade-off often proves mutually beneficial.

Settlement Agreement Documentation Requirements

Any negotiated settlement agreement must be properly documented to ensure that both parties understand their obligations while protecting you from future collection attempts on the same debt. Inadequate documentation of settlement agreements can result in continued collection efforts, credit reporting problems, and disputes about the terms that were actually agreed upon.

Essential Settlement Agreement Elements

Comprehensive settlement agreements should specify the exact debt being settled, including original creditor, account numbers, and claimed amounts. The agreement should clearly state the settlement amount and payment terms, specify that the settlement resolves the debt in its entirety, and include provisions preventing future collection attempts by the current collector or any successor.

Additionally, the agreement should address credit reporting issues, specifying whether the account will be reported as "settled" or whether the collector will request deletion of negative credit information. Include provisions requiring the collector to provide written confirmation of settlement completion and to cease all collection activities once payment terms are satisfied.

Sample Settlement Agreement Template

DEBT SETTLEMENT AGREEMENT

This Agreement is entered into between [Your Name] ("Consumer") and [Collector Name] ("Collector") regarding the debt described below.

Account Information:

- Original Creditor: [Original Creditor Name]
- Account Number: [Account Number]
- Claimed Balance: $[Amount]

Settlement Terms:

1. Consumer agrees to pay $[Settlement Amount] in [full payment/installments] to settle this account in its entirety.

1. Payment Schedule: [Specify payment amounts and due dates if installment agreement]

1. Upon receipt of the settlement payment(s), Collector agrees that this debt will be considered satisfied in full and will cease all collection activities.

1. Collector agrees not to pursue collection of any remaining balance and will not sell or assign any rights to collect this debt to any third party.

1. Credit Reporting: [Specify agreed-upon credit reporting treatment]

1. This agreement represents the complete understanding between the parties and supersedes any previous communications regarding this debt.

Consumer: ____________________ Date: ___________
[Your Signature]
Collector: ____________________ Date: ___________
[Collector Representative]
[Title]

Statutes of Limitations: Time as Your Ally

Among the most powerful protections available to consumers dealing with old debts, statutes of limitations create legal barriers that can completely eliminate collection liability for debts that exceed specific age limits. Understanding these time-based protections empowers you to challenge collection attempts that violate these fundamental limitations while avoiding actions that might inadvertently reset limitation periods.

Statutes of limitations for debt collection vary significantly among states and types of debt, creating a complex landscape that requires careful research and strategic application. However, the basic principle remains consistent across all jurisdictions: creditors and collectors must pursue legal remedies within specified time periods, or they lose their right to obtain court judgments that could result in wage garnishment or asset seizure.

Understanding Limitation Period Calculations

The calculation of limitation periods involves more complexity than simply counting years from the date an account became delinquent. Different triggering events may apply depending on the type of debt and the specific language of state statutes, while certain actions by either party can reset or extend limitation periods in ways that affect collection liability.

Most limitation periods begin running from the date of last activity on an account, which may be the last payment made, the last charge incurred, or the last acknowledgment of the debt by the consumer. However, some states calculate limitation periods from the date of contractual breach or the date the account was charged off by the original creditor, creating variations that require careful analysis of specific circumstances.

State-by-State Variations in Limitation Periods

Limitation periods range from as short as three years in some states to as long as fifteen years in others, with most states providing limitation periods between four and six years for common forms of consumer debt. Credit card debts, personal loans, and auto loans typically fall under general contract limitation periods, while other types of debt may be subject to specific limitation provisions.

Some states distinguish between written and oral contracts, providing longer limitation periods for debts based on written agreements. Additionally, certain types of debt, such as student loans or tax obligations, may be subject to different limitation periods or may not be subject to limitation periods at all.

Strategic Application of Limitation Defenses

When collection attempts to involve debts that may have exceeded applicable limitation periods, strategic application of limitation defenses requires careful analysis of the specific facts and circumstances surrounding each debt. This analysis must consider not only the age of the debt but also any actions that might have reset the limitation period or any special circumstances that might extend or suspend the limitation clock.

Researching Applicable Limitation Periods

Begin by determining the exact limitation period that applies to your specific debt in your state, considering both the type of debt and the specific statutory language that governs limitation calculations. Many states provide different limitation periods for different types of contracts or obligations, making precise classification essential for accurate limitation analysis.

Research whether your state's limitations are based on contractual breach, last payment, last activity, or charge-off dates, as this determination affects the calculation of when limitation periods expire. Additionally, determine whether your state recognizes any exceptions or extensions that might affect limitation calculations in your specific circumstances.

Limitation Defense Letter Template

When asserting limitation defenses, formal written communication provides the most effective method for putting collectors on notice that their collection attempts may violate applicable statutes of limitations. This communication should be clear and specific about the limitation defense while demanding that the collector cease collection activities on time-barred debts.

[Date]

[Collector Name and Address]

Re: Account Number [Account Number] - Statute of Limitations Defense

Dear Sir or Madam:

I am in receipt of your communication dated [Date] regarding the above-referenced account. This letter serves as formal notice that I dispute your right to collect this alleged debt based on the applicable statute of limitations.

Based on my research, this debt appears to have exceeded the [Number]-year limitation period provided by [State] [Statute Citation] for [Type of Contract/Debt]. According to available records, the last activity on this account occurred on approximately [Date], making this debt time-barred under applicable law.

Please be advised that:

1. I dispute any collection activities on this time-barred debt as violations of the Fair Debt Collection Practices Act and applicable state law.

1. Any attempt to collect this time-barred debt, including threats of legal action, may constitute deceptive and unfair collection practices.

1. I will consider any continued collection attempts as harassment and may pursue legal remedies available under federal and state consumer protection laws.

1. If you believe this debt has not exceeded applicable limitation periods, please provide specific documentation supporting your position, including the exact dates you believe are relevant for limitation calculations.

I demand that you immediately cease all collection activities regarding this account and confirm in writing that you will take no further action to collect this time-barred debt.

This communication is not an acknowledgment of any debt, and I specifically deny any liability for the claimed obligation.

Sincerely,

[Your Signature]

[Your Printed Name]

[Your Address]

SENT VIA CERTIFIED MAIL, RETURN RECEIPT REQUESTED

Advanced Legal Strategies and Tactical Applications

Beyond the fundamental tools of validation, negotiation, and limitation defenses, sophisticated debt management strategies employ advanced legal concepts and tactical applications that can provide additional protection and leverage in complex collection situations. These advanced strategies require deeper understanding of legal principles but can yield substantial benefits when properly applied.

Regulatory Complaint Strategies

Filing complaints with appropriate regulatory agencies creates official records of collection violations while potentially triggering investigations that result in penalties against collectors and remedial actions that benefit you. These complaints serve dual purposes: they may result in direct resolution of your specific situation while contributing to broader enforcement efforts that protect all consumers.

The Consumer Financial Protection Bureau (CFPB) maintains a comprehensive complaint database that tracks collection violations and can trigger regulatory investigations when patterns of violations emerge. State attorneys general offices often maintain similar complaint systems that focus on violations of state consumer protection laws, while licensing authorities can investigate violations that might result in license suspension or revocation for collection agencies.

Effective Regulatory Complaint Preparation

Successful regulatory complaints require comprehensive documentation of violations, clear explanations of how specific collector actions violated applicable laws, and specific requests for remedial action. Include copies of all relevant correspondence, recordings of telephone conversations where legally permissible, and detailed timelines that demonstrate patterns of violative behavior.

Focus complaints on specific legal violations rather than general dissatisfaction with collection efforts, as regulatory agencies prioritize complaints that allege clear violations of laws within their jurisdiction. Reference specific statutory provisions that were violated while providing factual evidence that supports your allegations.

Credit Reporting Strategic Challenges

Debt collection activities often involve credit reporting that can damage your credit profile long after the underlying debts are resolved. Strategic challenges to inaccurate or inappropriate credit reporting can result in improved credit scores while creating additional negotiation leverage with collectors who may prefer to avoid credit reporting disputes.

The Fair Credit Reporting Act provides specific procedures for challenging inaccurate credit information, including requirements that credit reporting agencies investigate disputes within thirty days and remove information they cannot verify as accurate. Additionally, the law requires that collectors who report information to credit agencies maintain reasonable procedures to ensure accuracy and respond appropriately to consumer disputes.

Strategic Credit Dispute Integration

Integrate credit reporting challenges into your overall debt management strategy by timing disputes to maximize their impact on both credit improvement and collection negotiation. Challenge inaccurate reporting before initiating settlement negotiations to demonstrate your knowledge of legal protections while creating additional incentives for collectors to reach reasonable agreements.

Use successful credit dispute outcomes as leverage in settlement negotiations by demonstrating your ability to effectively challenge inaccurate information while suggesting that collectors who fail to cooperate may face additional regulatory scrutiny of their credit reporting practices.

Documentation and Evidence Preservation

Throughout your debt management activities, maintain comprehensive documentation that preserves evidence of collector violations, supports your legal positions, and creates records that can be used in potential legal actions. This documentation serves as your primary evidence in disputes while demonstrating to collectors that you are serious about protecting your rights.

Comprehensive Documentation Systems

Develop systematic approaches to documenting all collection contacts, including dates, times, persons involved, and specific statements made during conversations. Record telephone conversations where legally permissible, or immediately document the substance of conversations in writing while details remain fresh in your memory.

Maintain copies of all correspondence, both sent and received, along with proof of delivery for important communications sent via certified mail. Create chronological files that allow easy reference to the development of collection activities and your responses to those activities.

Your Legal Action Plan: From Knowledge to Results

Transforming your understanding of legal protections into practical results requires systematic implementation of the strategies and procedures outlined in this chapter. Your legal action plan should be tailored to your specific circumstances while incorporating the fundamental principles that maximize protection and leverage in debt collection situations.

Phase 1: Assessment and Documentation (Week 1)

Comprehensive Debt Inventory and Legal Analysis

Begin by creating detailed inventories of all debts subject to collection activities, including original creditors, current collectors, claimed amounts, and relevant dates for limitation analysis. For each debt, research applicable statutes of limitations in your state while documenting any circumstances that might affect limitation calculations.

Analyze each debt for potential validation challenges, focusing on debts that have been sold or transferred multiple times, debts involving complex relationships between original creditors and collectors, and debts where you have reason to believe the claimed amounts are inaccurate or inflated.

Evidence Organization and Preservation

Organize all existing documentation related to debts under collection, including original agreements, payment records, collection correspondence, and credit reports. Create systematic filing methods that allow easy access to relevant documents while preserving evidence in formats suitable for potential legal proceedings.

Document any collection violations you have already experienced, including contacts outside permitted hours, discussions with third parties, threats of illegal actions, or demands for payments that exceed what you legally owe. This documentation provides foundation for potential legal action while demonstrating patterns of violative behavior.

Phase 2: Strategic Communication Implementation (Weeks 2-3)

Validation Request Deployment

Send comprehensive debt validation requests to all active collectors using certified mail with return receipt requested, ensuring that you meet the thirty-day deadline for validation requests while creating official records of your communications. Customize validation requests based on the specific circumstances of each debt while maintaining consistent approaches that maximize your protection.

Track responses to validation requests carefully, noting collectors who fail to respond within required timeframes, provide inadequate validation, or continue collection activities during validation periods. Document any violations of validation requirements as potential bases for legal action or regulatory complaints.

Credit Report Analysis and Dispute Initiation

Obtain current credit reports from all three major credit reporting agencies and identify any inaccurate information related to debts under collection. File formal disputes for inaccurate information using the procedures provided by credit reporting agencies while maintaining detailed records of dispute submissions and responses.

Coordinate credit disputes with validation requests to maximize pressure on collectors while creating multiple avenues for challenging inaccurate or unverifiable information. Use successful credit dispute outcomes as leverage in subsequent negotiations with collectors.

Phase 3: Negotiation and Resolution (Weeks 4-8)

Settlement Negotiation Implementation

Initiate settlement negotiations with collectors who have provided adequate validation or who have demonstrated legitimate collection authority, using the economic and timing principles discussed in this chapter. Begin negotiations from positions that reflect any weaknesses you discovered during validation while maintaining realistic expectations about achievable outcomes.

Document all negotiation communications in writing, either through written correspondence or through written confirmation of oral agreements. Avoid making commitments during initial negotiation discussions, instead requesting written confirmation of any proposed settlement terms before making final decisions.

Agreement Documentation and Compliance Monitoring

Ensure that all settlement agreements are properly documented using the templates and requirements outlined in this chapter, with specific attention to provisions that protect you from future collection attempts and adverse credit reporting. Review all agreement terms carefully before signing while ensuring that you understand all obligations and protections provided.

Monitor compliance with settlement agreements by both parties, ensuring that you make required payments on time while verifying that collectors honor their commitments regarding collection cessation and credit reporting. Document any violations of settlement agreements as potential bases for legal action or regulatory complaints.

Phase 4: Long-Term Protection and Monitoring (Ongoing)

Regulatory Complaint Filing

File complaints with appropriate regulatory agencies for any collection violations you documented during the process, using the complaint preparation strategies outlined in this chapter. Follow up on regulatory complaints to ensure they are being properly investigated while providing additional documentation if requested by regulatory agencies.

Use successful regulatory complaint outcomes as precedents for future collection disputes while building relationships with regulatory personnel who may be helpful in addressing future collection problems.

Ongoing Legal Education and Rights Maintenance

Stay informed about changes in consumer protection laws and collection industry practices that might affect your rights or create new opportunities for protection. Subscribe to consumer protection publications, follow relevant regulatory agency announcements, and maintain awareness of legal developments that could impact debt collection activities.

Build networks of other informed consumers who can provide support and advice in future collection situations while sharing your knowledge with others who may benefit from understanding their legal protections.

The Empowerment That Transforms Your Financial Future

As we conclude this comprehensive exploration of legal strategies for managing credit debt, remember that you now possess tools that have the power to fundamentally transform your relationship with debt collectors and your overall financial trajectory. The knowledge contained within this chapter represents years of legal development, countless court battles, and the accumulated wisdom of consumer advocates who fought to ensure that ordinary people like you would possess meaningful protections against financial exploitation.

Your mastery of these legal tools extends far beyond their immediate application to current debt situations. The confidence that comes from understanding your rights, the negotiation skills developed through strategic communication, and the documentation habits that support legal protection create permanent improvements in your financial capabilities that will benefit you throughout your life.

Every successful validation request strengthens your position in future collection disputes. Every well-negotiated settlement demonstrates your ability to achieve favorable outcomes through informed action. Every regulatory complaint contributes to broader enforcement efforts that protect all consumers from predatory practices.

Chapter Challenge: Activate Your Legal Protection System

This Week:

- Complete comprehensive debt inventory with limitation period analysis for each debt
- Send validation requests to all active collectors using certified mail
- Obtain current credit reports and identify inaccurate collection-related information
- Begin documenting any ongoing collection violations for potential regulatory complaints

This Month:

- Analyze validation responses and initiate settlement negotiations where appropriate
- File credit disputes for inaccurate collection-related information
- Research regulatory complaint procedures for any violations you have documented
- Begin building systematic documentation habits for all collection-related communications

This Quarter:

- Complete settlement negotiations for debts where validation was provided
- File regulatory complaints for any collection violations you have documented
- Monitor compliance with settlement agreements and credit dispute outcomes
- Share your knowledge with others who may benefit from understanding their legal protections

Remember that legal knowledge without action remains merely interesting information. The tools provided in this chapter require your active engagement to provide their full benefits, but the potential rewards—financial savings, improved credit, and lasting empowerment—justify every moment invested in their proper application.

Your wealth rebellion continues with every legal right you exercise, every unfair collection practice you challenge, and every moment you choose knowledge-based action over passive acceptance of unjust treatment. The legal system that once seemed designed to favor powerful creditors now serves as your protection and empowerment through your understanding of its principles and procedures.

In our next chapter, we will explore the complex world of retirement planning, discovering how to build long-term wealth through strategic approaches that transcend the limitations of traditional employer-sponsored plans. Because mastering current debt situations provides the foundation for building lasting prosperity that extends far beyond mere financial survival.

The chains of debt that once bound you are breaking through your understanding of the legal tools designed for your protection. Use this knowledge wisely, share it generously, and watch as your financial future transforms from one of vulnerability to one of strength, confidence, and lasting empowerment.

Chapter 8: US Codes That Protect You

"Knowledge of your rights is not merely academic—it is the armor that shields you from financial predators and the sword that cuts through deceptive practices. In the grand arena of personal finance, understanding the laws that protect you transforms you from prey into predator, from victim into victor."

Welcome, dear reader, to a chapter that will fundamentally transform your relationship with the financial systems that surround us. Here, within these pages, lies something far more valuable than investment advice or budgeting tips—you will discover the legal fortress that surrounds every American consumer, a shield forged by decades of legislative battles against those who would exploit the financially vulnerable.

As we embark on this journey together, I invite you to shed any notion that the law is too complex for ordinary people to understand or too distant to affect your daily life. The truth is quite the opposite: the legal protections we will explore were specifically designed for individuals like you, created by lawmakers who recognized that financial literacy must include legal literacy, and that true economic empowerment requires understanding not just how money works, but how the rules that govern money work as well.

This chapter represents your initiation into a select community—those who understand that financial freedom is not merely about accumulating wealth, but about protecting that wealth through the intelligent application of legal knowledge. You are about to discover that you possess far more power in financial transactions than you ever imagined, and that this power has been waiting patiently for you to claim it.

The Foundation of Financial Protection

In the vast landscape of American commerce, where trillions of dollars change hands daily through countless transactions, a complex web of federal and state laws works tirelessly to ensure that these exchanges occur fairly and transparently. These laws represent the accumulated wisdom of generations who learned, often through painful experience, that markets left entirely to their own devices inevitably produce systems that benefit the powerful at the expense of the vulnerable.

The financial protection laws we will explore emerged from real human suffering—families destroyed by predatory lending, individuals crushed by unfair debt collection practices, and countless Americans denied opportunities due to inaccurate credit reporting. Each law represents a victory won by ordinary citizens who refused to accept that financial exploitation was simply the price of participating in the American economy.

These protections exist not as abstract concepts studied in law school classrooms, but as practical tools designed for everyday use by people navigating car purchases, mortgage applications, credit card agreements, and countless other financial decisions. Understanding these tools empowers you to approach financial transactions with confidence, knowing that you possess both the knowledge to recognize unfair treatment and the legal authority to demand better.

The Architecture of Consumer Protection

The consumer protection framework operates on several levels simultaneously, creating multiple layers of defense against financial exploitation. Federal laws establish minimum standards that apply nationwide, while state laws often provide additional protections tailored to local circumstances and priorities. This layered approach ensures that regardless of where you live or what financial transaction you engage in, certain fundamental protections surround you.

At the federal level, agencies like the Consumer Financial Protection Bureau (CFPB), Federal Trade Commission (FTC), and various banking regulators enforce these laws with the authority to impose significant penalties on violators. These agencies possess the power to investigate complaints, conduct examinations of financial institutions, and take enforcement actions that can result in millions of dollars in fines and consumer restitution.

Yet the true power of these laws lies not in government enforcement alone, but in the private rights they create for individual consumers. Most consumer protection laws include provisions that allow you to take legal action against violators, often with the possibility of recovering attorney fees and damages that exceed your actual losses. This structure transforms every informed consumer into a potential enforcer of fair dealing standards.

The Fair Credit Reporting Act (FCRA): Your Shield Against Information Warfare

Your credit report represents one of the most important documents in your financial life, influencing your ability to secure housing, employment, insurance, and credit at reasonable terms. The Fair Credit Reporting Act, passed in 1970 and strengthened multiple times since, creates a comprehensive framework governing how credit information is collected, reported, and used, while providing you with powerful tools to ensure accuracy and protect your privacy.

The FCRA recognizes a fundamental truth that many consumers overlook: credit reporting agencies are not neutral record-keepers but profit-driven businesses that make money by selling information about you to other businesses. Without legal constraints, these agencies would have little incentive to prioritize accuracy or respect your privacy over their own profitability. The FCRA creates a carefully balanced system that allows legitimate business needs for credit information while protecting consumers from abuse.

Your FCRA Rights: A Comprehensive Arsenal

The FCRA grants you numerous specific rights that extend far beyond the commonly known right to receive free annual credit reports. Understanding the full scope of these rights empowers you to take control of your credit profile in ways that can dramatically improve your financial opportunities while protecting your privacy from unauthorized access.

The Right to Know Who Accesses Your Credit

Every time someone requests your credit report, the FCRA requires that this inquiry be recorded and made available to you. You have the right to know not only who has accessed your credit information but also when these accesses occurred and for what purpose. This transparency allows you to detect unauthorized inquiries that might indicate identity theft or inappropriate access by employers, landlords, or others who lack legitimate reasons for reviewing your credit.

This right proves particularly valuable when negotiating with potential creditors or landlords who might be hesitant to approve your applications. By reviewing your credit report before important applications, you can anticipate and address potential concerns while demonstrating to decision-makers that you actively monitor and manage your credit profile.

The Right to Dispute Inaccurate Information

Perhaps the most practically important FCRA right involves your ability to challenge inaccurate, incomplete, or outdated information on your credit reports. The law requires credit reporting agencies to investigate disputes within 30 days and to remove or correct information they cannot verify as accurate. This right extends beyond obvious errors to include information that may be technically accurate but misleading or unfairly prejudicial.

The dispute process, when properly utilized, can result in significant improvements to your credit score and financial opportunities. Many consumers carry unnecessarily damaged credit due to errors they never challenged, unaware that the law provides a straightforward mechanism for correction. Understanding how to effectively exercise this right can be worth thousands of dollars in lower interest rates and improved loan terms.

The Right to Add Explanatory Statements

When disputes cannot be resolved in your favor, the FCRA grants you the right to add 100-word explanatory statements to your credit report. These statements allow you to provide context for negative information that might otherwise be misunderstood by potential creditors or employers. While these statements don't directly improve credit scores, they can influence human decision-makers who review credit reports manually.

Effective explanatory statements focus on specific circumstances that led to credit problems while demonstrating current financial responsibility and commitment to meeting obligations. They prove particularly valuable for individuals who experienced temporary financial difficulties due to medical emergencies, job loss, or other circumstances beyond their control.

Real-World FCRA Applications

Understanding your FCRA rights becomes powerful only when combined with knowledge of how to exercise these rights effectively in practical situations. The following scenarios illustrate how strategic application of FCRA protections can produce tangible financial benefits and protect your interests in common situations.

Sarah's Credit Report Cleanup Success

Sarah discovered multiple errors on her credit report while preparing to apply for a mortgage, including accounts that didn't belong to her and payments incorrectly reported as late. Using her FCRA rights, she filed detailed disputes with all three credit reporting agencies, providing documentation that supported her claims. Within 30 days, the agencies removed the erroneous accounts and corrected the payment histories.

These corrections improved Sarah's credit score by 73 points, qualifying her for a mortgage interest rate that was 0.75% lower than she would have received with her previous score. Over the life of her 30-year mortgage, this improvement saved her approximately $43,000 in interest payments—a remarkable return on the time invested in understanding and exercising her FCRA rights.

Marcus's Employment Protection Strategy

When Marcus learned that a potential employer would be conducting a credit check as part of their hiring process, he proactively reviewed his credit report and discovered negative information related to a medical debt he had disputed with his insurance company. Rather than hoping the employer wouldn't notice or wouldn't care, Marcus added an explanatory statement detailing the insurance dispute and provided documentation showing his otherwise excellent credit management.

The employer appreciated Marcus's transparency and proactive approach to addressing the issue, ultimately offering him the position while noting that his explanation had been crucial in their decision. This demonstrates how understanding FCRA rights can transform potential vulnerabilities into demonstrations of responsibility and character.

The Truth in Lending Act (TILA): Illuminating the Real Cost of Credit

In the complex world of consumer credit, where marketing focuses on low monthly payments and attractive teaser rates while obscuring the true cost of borrowing, the Truth in Lending Act serves as a beacon of transparency. Enacted in 1968 and regularly updated to address new lending practices, TILA requires creditors to disclose credit terms clearly and consistently, enabling consumers to comparison shop and understand the real cost of credit before making commitments.

TILA recognizes that meaningful choice requires meaningful information, and that consumers cannot make rational decisions about credit without understanding both the total cost of borrowing and the terms that govern repayment. The law creates standardized disclosure requirements that cut through marketing confusion and legal complexity to provide clear, comparable information about credit offers.

TILA's Core Protections: Your Right to Financial Transparency

The Truth in Lending Act provides numerous protections that extend far beyond simple disclosure requirements, creating substantive rights that can save you thousands of dollars while protecting you from predatory lending practices. Understanding these protections empowers you to navigate credit markets with confidence while avoiding costly traps that ensnare uninformed borrowers.

Annual Percentage Rate (APR) Disclosure

TILA's most fundamental protection requires creditors to calculate and disclose the Annual Percentage Rate (APR) for all credit transactions using standardized methods that include not only interest charges but also most fees and costs associated with obtaining credit. This standardization allows you to compare credit offers from different lenders on an apples-to-apples basis, regardless of how those lenders structure their fees or marketing presentations.

The APR requirement proves particularly valuable when evaluating mortgage loans, where lenders may offer seemingly attractive interest rates while charging high origination fees, points, or other costs that significantly increase the true cost of borrowing. By comparing APRs rather than just interest rates, you can identify the genuinely best loan offers while avoiding high-cost loans disguised through creative fee structures.

The Right of Rescission

One of TILA's most powerful consumer protections provides a three-day cooling-off period for certain credit transactions, during which you can cancel the transaction for any reason without penalty. This right of rescission applies primarily to transactions where your home serves as collateral, recognizing that home equity represents most families' primary financial asset and deserves special protection from high-pressure sales tactics.

The rescission right must be clearly disclosed in writing, and the three-day period doesn't begin until you receive proper notice of this right. If creditors fail to provide proper rescission notices, your right to cancel can extend up to three years, providing powerful leverage in negotiations with lenders who violated disclosure requirements.

Billing Error Resolution Procedures

TILA establishes specific procedures for resolving billing errors on open-end credit accounts like credit cards and lines of credit. These procedures place the burden of proof on creditors to verify disputed charges while protecting you from collection efforts and negative credit reporting during the dispute process. Understanding these procedures can save you significant money while protecting your credit rating when billing disputes arise.

The law defines billing errors broadly to include charges for goods or services you didn't accept or that weren't delivered as agreed, mathematical errors, and charges for amounts different from what you agreed to pay. This broad definition provides protection against many forms of merchant fraud and error while ensuring that credit card companies cannot simply ignore legitimate disputes.

Strategic TILA Applications in Real-World Scenarios

The practical value of TILA protections becomes apparent when you understand how to apply these rights strategically in common financial situations. The following examples illustrate how informed consumers can use TILA protections to secure better deals, avoid costly mistakes, and resolve problems that arise in credit relationships.

David's Mortgage Shopping Success

When David decided to refinance his home mortgage, he received loan estimates from five different lenders, each presenting their offers using different terminology and fee structures that made comparison difficult. Rather than focusing on the interest rates or monthly payments emphasized in the lenders' marketing materials, David used his TILA knowledge to compare the APRs disclosed in the loan estimates.

This comparison revealed that the lender offering the lowest interest rate actually provided the highest total cost due to excessive fees, while another lender with a slightly higher interest rate offered the lowest APR and best overall value. By focusing on the standardized APR disclosures required by TILA, David saved approximately $8,400 over the life of his loan compared to the option that appeared most attractive based on marketing materials alone.

Lisa's Home Equity Loan Protection

Lisa signed a home equity loan agreement to fund home improvements, but immediately felt buyer's remorse after reading online reviews suggesting the lender engaged in predatory practices. Remembering her TILA rights, she reviewed her loan documents and confirmed that she had received proper rescission notices. She exercised her right to cancel the loan within the three-day rescission period, avoiding what would have been an expensive mistake.

The lender initially resisted her cancellation request, claiming that work had already begun on her home improvements. However, Lisa's understanding of TILA protections enabled her to insist on her legal rights, ultimately securing full cancellation of the loan without penalty. She subsequently obtained financing from a more reputable lender at terms that were significantly more favorable.

Lemon Laws: Your Defense Against Defective Products

While most consumer protection laws focus on financial services, state Lemon Laws provide crucial protections for one of the largest purchases most Americans make—motor vehicles. These laws recognize that cars represent both major financial investments and essential tools for employment, education, and daily life, deserving special protection when they fail to meet reasonable reliability expectations.

Lemon Laws vary significantly among states, but they share common principles: manufacturers must provide vehicles that meet basic reliability standards, and when vehicles experience substantial defects that cannot be repaired within a reasonable number of attempts, consumers deserve either replacement vehicles or full refunds. Understanding your state's specific Lemon Law provisions can save you thousands of dollars while ensuring that you receive the reliable transportation you paid for.

Universal Lemon Law Principles

Despite variations in specific requirements and procedures, most state Lemon Laws operate on similar principles that provide meaningful protection for consumers who purchase defective vehicles. Understanding these common elements empowers you to recognize when Lemon Law protections might apply to your situation while taking the documentation and procedural steps necessary to preserve your rights.

The Substantial Defect Requirement

Lemon Laws typically protect against substantial defects that significantly impair the vehicle's use, value, or safety, rather than minor cosmetic issues or problems that don't affect the vehicle's basic functionality. This standard recognizes that new vehicles may have minor imperfections that don't justify the drastic remedies of replacement or refund, while ensuring protection against serious problems that undermine the vehicle's fundamental purpose.

Substantial defects might include engine problems that cause stalling or loss of power, transmission failures that prevent proper shifting, electrical systems that cause safety hazards, or any combination of problems that collectively make the vehicle unreliable for normal use. The key is documenting how these defects impact your ability to use the vehicle safely and reliably.

The Reasonable Repair Opportunity Standard

Lemon Laws generally require that manufacturers be given reasonable opportunities to repair defects before consumers can seek replacement or refund remedies. This standard balances consumer rights with manufacturer interests, recognizing that complex products may sometimes experience problems that can be effectively repaired while ensuring that consumers don't remain stuck with persistently defective vehicles.

Most states define reasonable repair opportunities through specific numerical standards, such as three or four attempts to repair the same problem, or a certain number of days out of service for repairs. These bright-line rules provide clarity about when you've given the manufacturer sufficient opportunity to address problems and can pursue more substantial remedies.

Time and Mileage Limitations

Lemon Law protections typically apply only to vehicles purchased within certain time periods or mileage limits, recognizing that these laws are intended to protect against manufacturing defects rather than normal wear and tear that occurs with extended use. Most states provide protection for at least the first year of ownership or 12,000 miles, with many states offering longer protection periods.

Understanding these time and mileage limits proves crucial for preserving your rights, as Lemon Law remedies may not be available once these limits are exceeded. This makes early identification and documentation of problems essential for maintaining your legal options.

Maximizing Lemon Law Protection Through Strategic Documentation

The difference between successful and unsuccessful Lemon Law claims often depends not on the severity of the vehicle's problems, but on the quality of documentation maintained throughout the repair process. Understanding what to document and how to document it can mean the difference between recovering tens of thousands of dollars and being stuck with a defective vehicle.

Comprehensive Repair Documentation

Every interaction with dealership service departments should be thoroughly documented, including dates, descriptions of problems reported, work performed, parts replaced, and time the vehicle spent in the shop. This documentation serves as evidence that problems persist despite repair attempts and that the manufacturer has received adequate opportunity to address defects.

Effective documentation goes beyond simply keeping repair orders and receipts. Take photographs of any visible problems, maintain written records of conversations with service personnel, and document how problems affect your ability to use the vehicle safely and reliably. This comprehensive approach creates a compelling narrative that supports your Lemon Law claim.

The Power of Written Communication

While verbal complaints may initiate repair processes, written communication creates the formal documentation necessary for successful Lemon Law claims. Send written notices to manufacturers describing persistent problems and requesting resolution, keeping copies of all correspondence and proof of delivery. These written communications demonstrate that manufacturers have been properly notified of problems and given opportunities to address them.

Written communication also helps ensure that all parties understand the nature of problems and repair attempts, reducing the likelihood of miscommunication or disputes about what problems were reported and when. This clarity becomes essential when pursuing Lemon Law remedies that depend on demonstrating patterns of persistent problems.

Jennifer's Lemon Law Victory

Jennifer purchased a new sedan that immediately began experiencing electrical problems that caused the radio, air conditioning, and power windows to malfunction intermittently. The dealership attempted repairs five times over four months, replacing various components but never fully resolving the problems. Throughout this process, Jennifer maintained detailed documentation of each service visit, including photographs of malfunctioning components and written descriptions of how the problems affected her daily use of the vehicle.

When the problems persisted after the fifth repair attempt, Jennifer researched her state's Lemon Law and discovered that four unsuccessful repair attempts for the same problem qualified her for replacement or refund remedies. She submitted a formal Lemon Law claim supported by her comprehensive documentation, ultimately receiving a full refund of her purchase price plus attorney fees and costs. Her documentation proved crucial in demonstrating that the problems were substantial, persistent, and had been properly reported to the manufacturer.

Additional Federal Protections: Building Your Legal Arsenal

Beyond the major consumer protection laws we've explored, numerous additional federal statutes provide specific protections for various aspects of consumer financial transactions. Understanding these additional protections broadens your defensive capabilities while providing specialized tools for addressing particular types of problems that might arise in your financial dealings.

The Fair Debt Collection Practices Act (FDCPA): Your Shield Against Harassment

The Fair Debt Collection Practices Act protects consumers from abusive, deceptive, and unfair debt collection practices by third-party debt collectors. While the law doesn't eliminate your obligation to pay legitimate debts, it establishes clear boundaries for how debt collectors can attempt to collect those debts while providing you with powerful tools to stop harassment and abuse.

The FDCPA applies to third-party debt collectors—companies that collect debts owed to others—rather than original creditors collecting their own debts. However, many states have enacted similar protections that apply to original creditors as well, creating comprehensive protection against debt collection abuse regardless of who is attempting to collect the debt.

Prohibited Collection Practices

The FDCPA prohibits numerous specific collection practices that debt collectors commonly employed before the law's enactment. These prohibitions include calling before 8 AM or after 9 PM, contacting you at work if you've told them your employer prohibits such calls, discussing your debt with third parties, and using profane or abusive language.

Understanding these prohibitions empowers you to recognize when debt collectors violate the law while providing grounds for legal action that can result in damages and attorney fee awards. Many consumers tolerate abusive collection practices simply because they don't know these practices violate federal law and provide grounds for legal remedies.

Your Right to Verification and Dispute

Within five days of first contacting you, debt collectors must send written notices that include the amount of the debt, the name of the original creditor, and a statement of your right to dispute the debt within 30 days. If you dispute the debt in writing within this 30-day period, collectors must stop collection efforts until they provide verification that the debt is valid and belongs to you.

This verification requirement provides powerful protection against collection attempts for debts you don't owe, debts that have been paid, or debts for incorrect amounts. Many debt collection agencies purchase debts for pennies on the dollar without maintaining adequate documentation to prove the debts' validity, making the verification requirement an effective tool for challenging questionable collection attempts.

The Electronic Fund Transfer Act (EFTA): Digital Transaction Protection

As electronic transactions become increasingly common, the Electronic Fund Transfer Act provides essential protections for consumers who use debit cards, electronic bill payments, and other forms of electronic fund transfers. The law establishes clear rules for electronic transactions while providing error resolution procedures and limiting consumer liability for unauthorized transfers.

Limited Liability for Unauthorized Transactions

The EFTA limits your liability for unauthorized electronic fund transfers based on how quickly you report problems to your financial institution. If you report unauthorized transfers within two business days of discovering them, your liability is limited to $50. This protection encourages prompt reporting while ensuring that consumers don't bear unlimited liability for electronic fraud or errors.

Understanding these liability limits proves particularly important for consumers who use debit cards frequently or who conduct online banking transactions. Prompt reporting of problems can mean the difference between losing $50 and losing thousands of dollars to unauthorized transactions.

Error Resolution Procedures

Like TILA's billing error procedures for credit accounts, the EFTA establishes specific procedures for resolving errors in electronic fund transfers. Financial institutions must investigate reported errors within specific time frames while providing provisional credit for disputed amounts in many cases. These procedures protect consumers from being financially harmed while electronic transaction disputes are resolved.

Your Legal Protection Action Plan: From Knowledge to Power

Understanding consumer protection laws provides value only when combined with practical knowledge of how to exercise these rights effectively in real-world situations. Transforming legal knowledge into financial protection requires systematic approaches to documentation, communication, and enforcement that maximize your chances of successful outcomes.

Phase 1: Know Your Rights and Build Your Documentation System

Create a Consumer Rights Reference Guide

Develop a personal reference document that summarizes the key consumer protection laws that apply to your financial activities, including specific rights, time limits, and procedures for enforcement. This reference guide should be tailored to your state's laws and kept easily accessible for consultation when problems arise.

Include contact information for relevant regulatory agencies, such as your state attorney general's consumer protection division, the Consumer Financial Protection Bureau, and any state-specific agencies that enforce consumer protection laws. Having this information readily available enables quick action when problems arise.

Establish Documentation Systems

Create systematic approaches to documenting important financial transactions, including credit applications, major purchases, and any problems that arise with financial service providers. This documentation should include written records, photographs where appropriate, and copies of all relevant correspondence and agreements.

Digital tools can make documentation easier and more comprehensive than traditional paper-based systems. Consider using cloud-based storage solutions that automatically back up important documents while making them accessible from multiple devices. The key is creating systems that make documentation routine rather than burdensome.

Phase 2: Proactive Rights Exercise and Problem Prevention

Regular Credit Report Monitoring

Exercise your FCRA rights by obtaining and reviewing free credit reports from all three major credit reporting agencies at least annually, spreading these requests throughout the year to provide ongoing monitoring of your credit profile. Look for errors, unauthorized inquiries, and signs of identity theft that could affect your financial opportunities.

Consider setting up fraud alerts or credit freezes if you're concerned about identity theft, and understand the procedures for lifting these protections when you need to apply for credit legitimately. These proactive measures can prevent problems while demonstrating to creditors that you actively manage your credit profile.

Strategic Credit Shopping

When shopping for credit, use your TILA knowledge to compare offers based on APRs rather than just interest rates or monthly payments. Obtain written loan estimates or credit disclosures from multiple lenders and take time to review these documents carefully before making decisions.

Don't be pressured into making immediate decisions about credit offers, even when lenders suggest that terms are only available for limited periods. Legitimate lenders generally provide reasonable time for decision-making, and high-pressure tactics often indicate predatory lending practices you should avoid.

Phase 3: Effective Problem Resolution and Rights Enforcement

Systematic Complaint and Dispute Procedures

When problems arise, follow systematic approaches to complaint resolution that maximize your chances of successful outcomes while preserving your legal rights. Start with written complaints to the company involved, clearly describing the problem and the resolution you're seeking while referencing relevant consumer protection laws.

If direct complaints don't resolve problems, escalate to appropriate regulatory agencies while considering legal action for significant violations. Many consumer protection laws provide for attorney fee awards that make legal action economically viable even for relatively small disputes.

Documentation of Violations and Damages

When companies violate consumer protection laws, document both the violations and any damages you suffer as a result. These damages might include financial losses, time spent resolving problems, and emotional distress in cases involving harassment or other abusive practices.

Comprehensive damage documentation supports both regulatory complaints and potential legal action while ensuring that you receive appropriate compensation for violations. Many consumers settle for less than they deserve simply because they haven't adequately documented the full scope of their damages.

The Empowerment That Awaits Your Action

As we conclude this exploration of the legal protections that surround you, remember that knowledge without action remains merely interesting information. The laws we've discussed provide you with powerful tools for protection and empowerment, but these tools require your active engagement to provide their full benefits.

Your legal rights in financial transactions represent hard-won victories achieved by generations of consumers who refused to accept that exploitation was simply the price of participation in the American economy. These rights exist because ordinary people fought for them, and they remain effective only when ordinary people like you understand and exercise them.

The financial institutions, debt collectors, and other businesses you deal with possess sophisticated knowledge of relevant laws and regulations, often employing teams of lawyers to ensure their interests are protected. Your understanding of consumer protection laws helps level this playing field while ensuring that you can protect your interests with equal sophistication.

Chapter Challenge: Activate Your Legal Protections

This Week:

- Obtain free credit reports from all three major credit reporting agencies and review them for errors or signs of identity theft
- Research your state's specific Lemon Law provisions and other consumer protection laws that supplement federal protections
- Create a simple documentation system for financial transactions and begin using it consistently

This Month:

- Dispute any errors you discover on your credit reports using proper FCRA procedures
- Review recent credit offers or loan documents to ensure you understand all terms and that proper TILA disclosures were provided
- Create a consumer rights reference guide tailored to your state's laws and your financial activities

This Quarter:

- Exercise your right to free annual credit reports and compare current reports to previous versions to identify changes
- If you experience any consumer protection violations, file appropriate complaints with regulatory agencies and consider legal action for significant violations
- Share your knowledge of consumer protection laws with friends and family members, helping to build a community of informed consumers

Remember that your rights as a consumer exist not as abstract legal concepts, but as practical tools designed for everyday use by people like you. Every time you exercise these rights, you not only protect your own interests but also contribute to a marketplace culture that respects consumer protection and fair dealing.

Your wealth rebellion continues with every informed financial decision you make, every right you exercise to protect yourself from exploitation, and every moment you choose knowledge over ignorance in navigating the complex world of consumer finance. The laws are on your side—now it's time to put them to work for your financial future.

In our next chapter, we will explore specific strategies for applying these legal protections to credit and debt situations, transforming your theoretical knowledge into practical debt management and credit improvement tools. Because understanding your rights is powerful, but knowing exactly how to use those rights in specific situations makes you truly formidable in the financial arena.

The system that once kept you vulnerable through ignorance now serves as your protection through knowledge. Welcome to the empowered side of consumer finance, where understanding the rules transforms you from target into champion in the quest for financial freedom and security.

Chapter 9: The 401(k) Scam

"The 401(k) was never designed to be your primary retirement plan—it was created as a tax shelter for executives. Yet somehow, an entire generation has been convinced that this flawed system represents their only path to financial security. It's time to awaken from this collective delusion and reclaim control of your financial destiny."

Our money movement is advancing into its revealing stage. The 401(k) IS A SCAM! In this discussion, we delve into a realm that questions one of the most firmly held beliefs in American financial culture—the idea that the 401(k) is your best chance for a stable retirement. As we begin this investigation, I encourage you to consider these findings with an open mindset and the bravery to scrutinize what you've been taught about retirement planning.

The story we're about to uncover is one of institutional betrayal, where a system originally designed to benefit corporate executives has been repackaged and sold to ordinary workers as their salvation. It is a tale of how complexity has been weaponized against the very people it claims to serve, and how the promise of employer matching has been used to mask a web of fees, restrictions, and limitations that drain wealth from those who can least afford it.

This chapter represents your invitation into a select community of informed individuals who understand that true financial security comes not from surrendering control of your money to corporate-sponsored plans, but from taking deliberate ownership of your retirement destiny through superior alternatives that put you, rather than financial institutions, in the driver's seat of your future prosperity.

The Great 401(k) Deception: How We Got Here

To understand the magnitude of the 401(k) deception, we must first explore the historical accident that transformed a tax loophole for wealthy executives into the primary retirement system for millions of American workers. This transformation represents one of the most successful marketing campaigns in financial history—convincing ordinary people that a system designed to benefit the wealthy would somehow serve their interests as well.

The 401(k) emerged in 1978 as Section 401(k) of the Internal Revenue Code, originally intended as a narrow provision allowing executives to defer a portion of their compensation in a tax-advantaged manner. The architects of this legislation never envisioned it replacing traditional pension plans or becoming the primary retirement vehicle for entire generations of workers. Yet through a combination of corporate cost-cutting initiatives and aggressive marketing by the financial services industry, this executive tax shelter evolved into the retirement system that now governs the financial futures of over 100 million Americans.

The transition from traditional pension plans to 401(k)-based systems represents one of the greatest transfers of risk and responsibility from institutions to individuals in modern financial history. Under traditional pension systems, employers bore the investment risk and guaranteed specific retirement benefits regardless of market performance. The shift to 401(k) plans transferred this risk entirely to employees, who now bear full responsibility for investment decisions, market volatility, and the adequacy of their retirement savings—often without the knowledge or resources necessary to succeed in this complex endeavor.

The Illusion of Employer Generosity

The 401(k) system has been masterfully marketed as a generous employee benefit, with employer matching contributions positioned as "free money" that employees would be foolish to refuse. This framing obscures the reality that employer contributions are simply deferred compensation—money that rightfully belongs to employees but is being held hostage by restrictions, fees, and vesting schedules that benefit employers and financial services companies more than the workers themselves.

Consider the true economics of employer matching: companies that offer 401(k) matches typically provide 50 cents for every dollar contributed, up to a certain percentage of salary. This "50% return" sounds attractive until you realize that the match is often subject to vesting schedules that can span several years, meaning you forfeit these contributions if you change jobs before becoming fully vested. Additionally, both your contributions and the employer match are immediately subject to the fees and restrictions that make 401(k) plans so profitable for the financial services industry.

The marketing of employer matching as "free money" also ignores the opportunity cost of the restrictions placed on your funds. When you contribute to a 401(k), you surrender control of your money to plan administrators who limit your investment choices, charge fees for basic transactions, and impose penalties for accessing your own funds before age 59½. These restrictions would be unacceptable in any other financial context, yet they are presented as reasonable trade-offs for the privilege of receiving employer contributions.

The Complexity Weapon

One of the most insidious aspects of the 401(k) system is its deliberate complexity, which serves to obscure the true costs and limitations while making it difficult for participants to make informed decisions about their retirement savings. This complexity is not accidental—it is a carefully crafted feature that allows financial services companies to extract maximum fees while minimizing participant awareness of these costs.

The typical 401(k) plan document runs hundreds of pages and contains language so technical and convoluted that even financial professionals struggle to understand all the terms and conditions. Participants are expected to navigate investment menus containing dozens of mutual funds with cryptic names and varying fee structures, often without adequate information to make informed choices about their long-term financial security.

This complexity extends to fee disclosure, where plan costs are buried in layers of documentation and expressed using terminology that obscures their true impact on retirement wealth. A fee that seems modest when expressed as a percentage can represent tens of thousands of dollars in lost wealth over a career, yet the compounding effect of these fees is rarely explained to participants in terms they can understand.

The Hidden Fee Assault: Death by a Thousand Cuts

Perhaps no aspect of the 401(k) system is more deceptive than its fee structure, which operates like a sophisticated wealth extraction machine designed to siphon money from participant accounts while maintaining the illusion of low-cost investing. These fees work silently and relentlessly, compounding their negative impact over decades to create wealth transfers that can exceed the contributions made by many participants.

The fee assault begins with administrative costs that are often invisible to participants but embedded in the expense ratios of investment options or deducted directly from account balances. These fees cover everything from recordkeeping and customer service to compliance and marketing expenses, transforming every participant into an unwilling contributor to the profit margins of financial services companies.

The Expense Ratio Trap

At the heart of 401(k) fee extraction lies the expense ratio trap, where seemingly modest annual fees compound over time to create devastating impacts on retirement wealth. An expense ratio of 1% might sound reasonable, but this annual charge represents a massive wealth transfer over a typical career span that few participants fully understand.

Consider Maria, who contributes $6,000 annually to her 401(k) for 30 years, earning an average return of 7% before fees. With a 1% expense ratio, her account would grow to approximately $566,000. However, if she could invest the same money with a 0.1% expense ratio, her account would reach approximately $677,000—a difference of $111,000 created entirely by fee differences. This $111,000 represents nearly 19 years of Maria's contributions, effectively transferring almost two decades of her savings to financial services companies.

The expense ratio trap becomes even more insidious when you realize that many 401(k) plans offer investment options with expense ratios significantly higher than 1%, sometimes reaching 2% or more for actively managed funds that typically underperform low-cost index alternatives. These high-fee options are often marketed as providing superior professional management, yet study after study demonstrates that high-fee actively managed funds rarely justify their costs through improved performance.

Hidden Trading Costs and Revenue Sharing

Beyond the visible expense ratios lie additional fee layers that further erode participant wealth through trading costs, revenue sharing arrangements, and other charges that rarely appear in participant statements. These hidden fees can add another 0.5% to 1% in annual costs, doubling the true expense of 401(k) participation while remaining largely invisible to the participants who pay them.

Revenue sharing represents one of the most deceptive aspects of 401(k) fee structures, where mutual fund companies pay portions of their management fees back to plan administrators and recordkeepers in exchange for inclusion in investment menus. These arrangements create conflicts of interest where plan fiduciaries may select investment options based on the revenue they generate rather than their suitability for participants.

The existence of revenue sharing means that participants often pay twice for the same services—once through visible plan administration fees and again through the hidden fees embedded in investment options. This double payment structure enriches plan providers while depleting retirement accounts, creating a system where the interests of service providers are directly opposed to the interests of the participants they are supposed to serve.

The Loan and Withdrawal Fee Bonanza

The 401(k) system generates additional fee revenue through charges imposed when participants attempt to access their own money through loans or hardship withdrawals. These fees transform what should be routine account management into profit centers for plan providers, creating perverse incentives to complicate and restrict access to participant funds.

Loan fees typically include origination charges, annual maintenance fees, and processing costs that can total hundreds of dollars for the privilege of borrowing your own money. These fees are particularly egregious because they are charged for administrative functions that cost plan providers minimal amounts to perform, yet they are presented as necessary charges for providing participant services.

Hardship withdrawal fees add insult to injury by charging participants who are experiencing financial emergencies additional costs for accessing their retirement funds. These fees, combined with early withdrawal penalties and tax consequences, create multiple layers of punishment for participants who need to access their savings during difficult periods.

Employer Control: Your Money, Their Rules

The 401(k) system grants employers unprecedented control over their workers' retirement savings, creating a power dynamic that serves corporate interests while limiting participant flexibility and autonomy. This control extends far beyond simple plan administration, encompassing investment choices, timing of contributions, and even the ability to access funds during employment.

Employers exercise this control through plan design decisions that prioritize corporate objectives over participant welfare, often selecting service providers and investment options based on cost minimization or revenue sharing arrangements rather than participant outcomes. This structural misalignment of interests ensures that 401(k) plans serve corporate balance sheets more effectively than they serve participant retirement security.

Investment Menu Manipulation

One of the most significant ways employers control participant outcomes is through the curation of investment menus that limit choices to options approved by plan sponsors and their advisors. These menus often exclude low-cost index funds that would provide superior long-term returns in favor of high-fee actively managed options that generate more revenue for plan providers.

The typical 401(k) investment menu contains 15-20 mutual fund options selected not for their potential to build participant wealth, but for their ability to satisfy various risk and return categories while generating acceptable revenue streams for plan administrators. This curated selection process eliminates many of the best investment options available in the broader market, forcing participants to choose from a limited set of alternatives that may not align with their investment objectives or risk tolerance.

Even when low-cost index options are included in 401(k) menus, they are often buried among numerous high-fee alternatives or presented with confusing names and descriptions that obscure their advantages. This deliberate obfuscation steers participants toward higher-fee options that increase plan profitability while reducing participant returns.

Contribution Timing and Matching Manipulation

Employers further control participant outcomes through policies governing contribution timing and matching calculations that can significantly impact the effective return on employee savings. Many companies impose delays between employee contributions and employer matches, reducing the compounding period for matching funds and creating cash flow benefits for employers at participant expense.

Some employers calculate matching contributions based on pay periods rather than annual amounts, creating situations where participants who contribute unevenly throughout the year may forfeit portions of available matches. These calculation methods, while technically disclosed in plan documents, are rarely explained clearly to participants and can result in thousands of dollars in lost matching contributions over a career.

The timing of matching contributions also affects participant outcomes, as employers may delay match deposits until the end of the plan year rather than making them contemporaneously with employee contributions. This delay reduces the compounding period for matching funds while providing employers with interest-free use of money that belongs to participants.

Vesting Schedules: Employer Insurance Policies

Perhaps the most egregious example of employer control over participant funds is the use of vesting schedules that allow companies to recapture their matching contributions from employees who leave before completing specified service periods. These schedules function as employer insurance policies, reducing the true cost of matching contributions while increasing employee retention through financial penalties for job changes.

Vesting schedules typically span three to six years, with participants gradually earning rights to employer contributions over this period. During this time, employer matches are held hostage, creating golden handcuffs that discourage job mobility and limit career advancement opportunities for participants who cannot afford to forfeit unvested contributions.

The economic impact of vesting schedules extends beyond direct forfeiture of employer contributions to include opportunity costs associated with staying in unsuitable positions to preserve retirement benefits. Young workers, who benefit most from job mobility and career advancement, are particularly harmed by vesting schedules that prioritize employer retention goals over participant career development.

Inflation: The Silent Wealth Destroyer

While 401(k) participants focus on account balance growth and employer matching contributions, inflation works silently to erode the purchasing power of their retirement savings in ways that are rarely explained or understood. This erosion occurs gradually over decades, making it difficult for participants to recognize the true impact until they approach retirement and discover that their accumulated savings provide far less financial security than anticipated.

The relationship between 401(k) accumulation and inflation protection is particularly problematic because traditional contribution limits and investment options provide inadequate tools for maintaining purchasing power over multi-decade accumulation periods. Unlike other investment vehicles that can be adjusted dynamically to respond to changing economic conditions, 401(k) plans lock participants into contribution limits and investment menus that may become obsolete as economic conditions evolve.

The Purchasing Power Erosion

Historical inflation rates average approximately 3% annually over long periods, meaning that money doubles in cost roughly every 23 years. For young workers beginning their careers today, this inflation rate suggests that their retirement expenses could be four to eight times higher than current levels, requiring account balances that far exceed what seems adequate based on today's purchasing power.

The problem is compounded by healthcare inflation, which typically exceeds general inflation rates and represents one of the largest expense categories for retirees. Healthcare costs have increased at rates of 5-7% annually over recent decades, suggesting that healthcare expenses alone could consume disproportionate shares of retirement savings accumulated through traditional 401(k) plans.

Consider David, who accumulates $1 million in his 401(k) over a 40-year career. While $1 million sounds substantial, 3% annual inflation would reduce its purchasing power to approximately $307,000 in today's money. If healthcare inflation averages 6% annually, his healthcare purchasing power would be even more dramatically eroded, potentially leaving him financially vulnerable despite decades of diligent saving.

Fixed Contribution Limit Inadequacy

The 401(k) system imposes annual contribution limits that are adjusted periodically for inflation but often lag behind actual cost increases and may be inadequate for participants who recognize late in their careers that they need to accelerate retirement savings. These limits create artificial constraints on accumulation that can prevent participants from achieving retirement security even when they have the income and motivation to save more aggressively.

For high-earning participants who maximize 401(k) contributions throughout their careers, these limits become particularly constraining as they approach retirement. A participant earning $200,000 annually can contribute only a small percentage of their income to 401(k) plans, potentially requiring decades longer to achieve retirement security than would be necessary with more flexible contribution vehicles.

The interaction between contribution limits and inflation also creates problems for participants whose income growth exceeds inflation rates. As their earning power increases, the fixed nature of contribution limits means that 401(k) savings represent declining percentages of their income, potentially leaving them with inadequate replacement ratios despite maximizing contributions within plan limits.

The Roth IRA Revolution: Taking Back Control

In stark contrast to the restrictions and fee structures that characterize 401(k) plans, Roth IRAs represent a revolutionary approach to retirement savings that prioritizes participant control, investment flexibility, and tax-free growth over the institutional priorities that drive traditional employer-sponsored plans. This alternative retirement vehicle provides nearly everything that 401(k) plans lack: complete investment control, unlimited investment options, fee transparency, and tax-free withdrawals in retirement.

The Roth IRA structure embodies principles of financial independence that directly counter the dependency relationships created by 401(k) plans. Rather than surrendering control of your retirement savings to employers and plan administrators, Roth IRAs allow you to maintain complete autonomy overinvestment decisions while building wealth that will be entirely tax-free in retirement.

The Tax-Free Advantage

The most powerful feature of Roth IRAs lies in their tax treatment, which allows contributions made with after-tax dollars to grow completely tax-free for life. This tax treatment provides certainty about your tax obligations in retirement while protecting your savings from future tax rate increases that could significantly impact 401(k) withdrawals.

Unlike traditional 401(k) plans, where every dollar withdrawn in retirement is subject to ordinary income tax rates, Roth IRA withdrawals are completely tax-free after age 59½. This difference becomes increasingly significant as account balances grow, potentially saving hundreds of thousands of dollars in taxes over a typical retirement period.

The tax-free nature of Roth IRA growth also provides superior estate planning benefits, as inherited Roth IRAs can continue growing tax-free for beneficiaries while traditional retirement accounts impose immediate tax liabilities on heirs. This feature makes Roth IRAs powerful wealth transfer vehicles that can benefit multiple generations while avoiding the tax complications associated with traditional retirement accounts.

Complete Investment Freedom

Roth IRAs provide access to virtually every investment option available in financial markets, from individual stocks and bonds to real estate investment trusts, commodities, and alternative investments. This freedom allows you to construct portfolios tailored precisely to your risk tolerance, return objectives, and investment philosophy without the restrictions imposed by employer-curated investment menus.

The investment flexibility of Roth IRAs becomes particularly valuable for sophisticated investors who understand market dynamics and want to pursue strategies unavailable within 401(k) plans. Whether you prefer low-cost index investing, individual stock selection, or alternative investments like REITs and commodities, Roth IRAs provide the flexibility to implement these strategies without restriction.

This investment freedom also allows for dynamic portfolio management that responds to changing market conditions and life circumstances. Unlike 401(k) plans that lock you into predetermined investment menus for entire career spans, Roth IRAs can be adjusted continuously to optimize for changing objectives and market opportunities.

Fee Transparency and Control

Roth IRAs eliminate the complex fee structures that characterize 401(k) plans, providing complete transparency about investment costs while allowing you to minimize expenses through strategic provider and investment selection. Rather than being forced to accept the fee structures imposed by employer-selected plan providers, Roth IRA owners can shop for the lowest-cost providers and investment options available in the marketplace.

The fee differences between Roth IRAs and 401(k) plans can be substantial, particularly for investors who choose low-cost index funds through discount brokers. While 401(k) participants often pay total fees exceeding 1.5% annually, Roth IRA investors can construct diversified portfolios with total costs below 0.1%, creating fee savings that compound dramatically over multi-decade accumulation periods.

This fee control becomes even more important as account balances grow, since percentage-based fees represent larger dollar amounts on substantial balances. A 1% fee on a $500,000 account costs $5,000 annually, while a 0.1% fee costs only $500—a difference of $4,500 per year that compounds over time to create enormous wealth preservation differences.

Solo Retirement Accounts: The Entrepreneur's Secret Weapon

For self-employed individuals and business owners, solo retirement accounts provide access to contribution limits and tax benefits that far exceed what's available through traditional employee plans. These accounts combine the investment flexibility and fee control of IRAs with contribution limits that can reach $66,000 annually for 2023, creating powerful wealth-building opportunities for entrepreneurs and freelancers.

Solo 401(k) plans, also known as individual 401(k) or one-participant 401(k) plans, allow business owners to contribute both as employees and employers, effectively doubling their tax-advantaged retirement savings capacity compared to traditional employee plans. This structure provides particular benefits for high-earning self-employed individuals who want to maximize their tax-deferred retirement savings while maintaining complete control over investment decisions.

Maximizing Contribution Potential

The contribution structure of solo retirement accounts allows eligible participants to contribute up to $22,500 as an employee (for 2023) plus up to 25% of their business income as an employer contribution, with total contributions capped at $66,000 annually. For participants over age 50, catch-up contributions increase these limits to $73,500 annually, providing substantial acceleration opportunities for retirement savings.

These higher contribution limits become particularly valuable for business owners whose income varies significantly from year to year. During high-income years, solo retirement accounts allow maximum tax-deferred savings that can offset business income and reduce tax liabilities while building retirement security. During lower-income years, reduced contributions can help preserve cash flow for business operations.

The flexibility to adjust contributions based on business performance also provides tax planning opportunities unavailable to traditional employees. Business owners can time contributions to optimize their tax situations while building retirement wealth at accelerated rates compared to traditional employment relationships.

Complete Administrative Control

Solo retirement accounts provide complete administrative control over plan features, investment options, and operational procedures, eliminating the conflicts of interest and service provider limitations that characterize employer-sponsored plans. This control allows business owners to optimize their retirement plans for their specific objectives rather than accepting compromises imposed by group plan requirements.

Administrative control extends to service provider selection, where solo account owners can choose custodians and investment platforms based purely on cost and service quality rather than accepting providers selected by employers based on other criteria. This freedom often results in lower fees and superior service compared to employer-sponsored alternatives.

The administrative simplicity of solo accounts also reduces compliance burdens compared to employer-sponsored plans, particularly for businesses with only owner-employees. While larger employer plans require extensive documentation, testing, and reporting, solo accounts operate with minimal administrative requirements that can be managed by business owners or their accountants without specialized plan administration services.

Building Your Retirement Liberation Strategy

Creating a retirement strategy that prioritizes your interests over institutional profits requires systematic analysis of your options and deliberate action to implement superior alternatives to traditional employer-sponsored plans. This liberation strategy begins with understanding your specific circumstances and objectives, then proceeds through evaluation of available options to implementation of approaches that maximize your wealth-building potential while minimizing fees and restrictions.

Your retirement liberation strategy should be built upon principles of control, cost minimization, tax optimization, and flexibility that enable you to adapt your approach as circumstances change throughout your career and life. Rather than accepting the limitations imposed by employer-sponsored plans, this strategy empowers you to create retirement security through informed choices and strategic implementation.

Phase 1: 401(k) Audit and Analysis

Begin your retirement liberation by conducting a comprehensive audit of any existing 401(k) participation, focusing on total fees, investment performance, and restrictions that may be limiting your wealth-building potential. This audit should quantify the true cost of your current approach while identifying specific areas where alternative strategies could provide superior outcomes.

Document all fees associated with your 401(k) participation, including expense ratios, administrative fees, and transaction costs that may be deducted from your account. Calculate the annual dollar cost of these fees based on your current account balance and project their impact over your remaining working years to understand the total wealth erosion created by fee structures.

Evaluate your current investment allocation within your 401(k) against low-cost alternatives available outside the plan, focusing on expense ratio differences and performance comparisons that reveal the opportunity cost of restricted investment options. This analysis often reveals substantial potential improvements in returns through investment approach changes.

Phase 2: Alternative Strategy Implementation

Based on your 401(k) audit results, develop specific strategies for minimizing plan participation while maximizing alternative retirement savings approaches that provide superior wealth-building potential. This may involve reducing 401(k) contributions to the minimum level required to capture available employer matching while directing additional retirement savings to Roth IRAs or other alternatives.

For self-employed individuals or those with consulting income, explore solo retirement account options that provide higher contribution limits and complete investment control. These accounts often provide superior wealth-building opportunities compared to employee plans while eliminating many of the restrictions and fees that limit 401(k) effectiveness.

Consider the tax implications of your alternative strategy implementation, particularly the trade-offs between current tax deductions available through traditional retirement accounts and future tax-free withdrawals provided by Roth alternatives. This analysis should consider your current tax bracket, expected retirement tax situation, and potential changes in tax policy that could affect different retirement account types.

Phase 3: Optimization and Monitoring

Once you've implemented alternative retirement strategies, establish systems for ongoing optimization and monitoring that ensure your approach continues to serve your objectives as circumstances change. This includes regular review of investment performance, fee structures, and contribution strategies that may need adjustment based on changes in income, tax laws, or retirement objectives.

Create annual review processes that compare your alternative strategy performance against the 401(k) option you've modified or replaced, quantifying the benefits of your liberation approach through concrete performance and cost comparisons. This documentation reinforces the wisdom of your strategy choices while identifying areas for further optimization.

Monitor changes in retirement account regulations and tax law that may create new opportunities or require adjustments to your strategy. The retirement planning landscape evolves continuously, and staying informed about new options ensures that your liberation strategy remains optimized for current opportunities.

Your Retirement Revolution Action Plan

Transforming your retirement planning from dependency on flawed employer-sponsored systems to independent wealth building requires specific actions that implement the principles and strategies outlined in this chapter. Your retirement revolution begins with education and analysis, progresses through strategic implementation, and continues with ongoing optimization that ensures long-term success.

Immediate Action Items (This Week)

Complete 401(k) Fee Analysis

Obtain complete fee disclosure documents for any 401(k) plans in which you currently participate, focusing on total annual costs including expense ratios, administrative fees, and any additional charges that reduce your returns. Calculate the annual dollar cost of these fees based on your current balance and project their impact over your expected working years.

Research Alternative Account Options

Investigate Roth IRA providers and investment options available outside your employer's plan, focusing on total costs and investment flexibility that could improve your wealth-building outcomes. Compare expense ratios for similar investments inside and outside your 401(k) to quantify potential savings from alternative approaches.

Evaluate Solo Account Eligibility

If you have any self-employment income or consulting revenue, research solo 401(k) and SEP-IRA options that may provide higher contribution limits and better investment control than traditional employee plans. Even modest self-employment income can qualify for these superior retirement savings vehicles.

Strategic Implementation (This Month)

Open Alternative Retirement Accounts

Open Roth IRA accounts with low-cost providers that offer the investment options and service quality you prefer, positioning these accounts to receive redirected retirement savings that might otherwise go to restrictive employer plans. Choose providers based on total costs, investment options, and service quality rather than marketing or convenience factors.

Adjust 401(k) Participation Strategy

If your analysis reveals high fees or poor investment options in your employer's plan, consider reducing contributions to the minimum level required to capture any employer matching while directing additional retirement savings to superior alternatives. This strategy maintains access to employer contributions while minimizing exposure to plan limitations.

Implement Investment Strategy

Develop and implement investment strategies for your alternative retirement accounts that take advantage of the flexibility and low costs unavailable in employer plans. This might include low-cost index fund portfolios, individual stock positions, or alternative investments that align with your risk tolerance and return objectives.

Long-Term Optimization (Ongoing)

Annual Performance Reviews

Conduct annual reviews comparing the performance of your alternative retirement strategies against your previous 401(k) approach, documenting the benefits of your liberation strategy through concrete return and cost comparisons. Use these reviews to make adjustments that optimize your approach for changing circumstances.

Contribution Strategy Updates

Regularly evaluate your contribution allocation between different account types based on changes in income, tax situations, and retirement objectives. As your circumstances evolve, the optimal mix of traditional and Roth contributions may change, requiring strategic adjustments to maintain optimization.

Investment Portfolio Rebalancing

Maintain and rebalance your retirement investment portfolios according to your strategic objectives and market conditions, taking advantage of the flexibility provided by alternative accounts to optimize for changing market environments and life circumstances.

The Freedom That Awaits Your Decision

As we conclude this revelatory exploration of 401(k) limitations and superior alternatives, remember that you now possess knowledge that can fundamentally transform your retirement outcomes and financial independence trajectory. The strategies we've discussed aren't theoretical concepts but practical approaches that have enabled countless individuals to build substantially more retirement wealth while maintaining greater control over their financial futures.

Your decision to move beyond traditional 401(k) dependency represents more than just a change in retirement savings strategy—it embodies a fundamental shift toward financial independence and personal empowerment that will benefit you throughout your life. Every dollar you redirect from high-fee employer plans to low-cost alternatives compounds over decades to create wealth differences that can mean the difference between financial stress and complete independence in retirement.

The path forward requires courage to challenge conventional wisdom and take responsibility for your own financial success, but the rewards justify every moment invested in this transformation. While others remain trapped in systems designed to enrich institutions at their expense, you will be building wealth through approaches optimized entirely for your benefit.

Chapter Challenge: Launch Your Retirement Revolution

This Week:

- Complete a comprehensive analysis of all fees in any current 401(k) participation
- Research and compare Roth IRA providers and investment options
- Calculate the long-term impact of fee differences between employer plans and alternatives
- If eligible, investigate solo retirement account options for any self-employment income

This Month:

- Open Roth IRA accounts with low-cost providers offering optimal investment options
- Adjust 401(k) participation to minimize high-fee exposure while maintaining employer matching
- Implement investment strategies that take advantage of your new account flexibility
- Create systems for ongoing monitoring and optimization of your retirement strategy

This Year:

- Document the performance improvements achieved through your retirement liberation strategy
- Educate others about 401(k) limitations and alternative approaches to retirement planning
- Continue optimizing your investment allocation and contribution strategies based on changing circumstances
- Build additional income sources that qualify for solo retirement account contributions

Remember that retirement security is not achieved through hoping that flawed systems will somehow provide adequate outcomes, but through taking control of your financial destiny using superior tools and strategies. Your retirement revolution begins with your decision to reject institutional dependency in favor of personal empowerment and strategic wealth building.

Your wealth rebellion continues with every dollar you redirect from expensive, restrictive employer plans to flexible, low-cost alternatives that prioritize your interests over institutional profits. The difference between financial dependency and complete independence often lies in the retirement planning decisions you make today.

In our next chapter, we will explore additional retirement account strategies that can accelerate your wealth building while providing even greater tax advantages and flexibility. Because understanding 401(k) limitations is just the beginning—true retirement security comes from mastering the full spectrum of retirement planning tools available to informed individuals.

The system that promised to take care of your retirement was designed to take care of itself first. Now that you understand this truth, you can build a retirement strategy that puts your interests first, where they belong. Welcome to retirement planning that actually works—for you.

Chapter 10: Financial Literacy for Neurodivergent Learners—Adaptive Wealth Systems

> *"Your neurological wiring is not a barrier to wealth—it is your unique pathway to financial sovereignty. In a world designed for neurotypical minds, your adaptive systems become acts of rebellion, transforming difference into advantage and creating wealth-building approaches that honor the beautiful complexity of your authentic self."*

See neurodiversity as a strength when building wealth. This chapter changes how we view neurodivergent minds, recognizing them not as challenges, but as powerful tools that need specific support to reach their full potential and achieve lasting financial success.

As we venture together into this empowering exploration, I invite you to release any shame or frustration you may have experienced with traditional financial systems that never quite fit the way your mind processes information. Instead, embrace the profound truth that emerges from these teachings: your neurodivergent brain possesses unique strengths and perspectives that, when properly supported with adaptive systems, can create extraordinary financial success.

This chapter serves as your comprehensive blueprint for building wealth in alignment with your neurological authenticity, transforming the very traits that others might see as limitations into powerful advantages that drive sustainable prosperity. Together, we will explore how to design financial systems that feel intuitive rather than overwhelming, create habits that build momentum through micro-actions, and develop an empowering identity as a neurodivergent wealth creator who builds success on their own terms.

Visual Systems, Micro-Actions & Habit Stacking: Building Your Financial Ecosystem

The neurodivergent mind often processes information through unique pathways that traditional financial education ignores, creating unnecessary barriers between you and the wealth-building knowledge that could transform your life. Visual learning, pattern recognition, and systematic approaches become powerful tools when properly harnessed through intentional design.

Understanding how your mind naturally organizes and retains information enables the creation of financial systems that feel effortless rather than overwhelming, working with your neurological wiring instead of fighting against it. This approach transforms financial management from a source of stress into a source of empowerment and clarity.

These adaptive systems recognize that success comes not from forcing yourself into neurotypical molds but from creating personalized approaches that honor your unique cognitive strengths while addressing areas that may need additional support through thoughtful system design.

Visual Systems for Clarity and Control

Color-coded budgeting systems tap into the brain's natural ability to process visual information more efficiently than numerical data alone, creating immediate understanding of financial categories and status through intuitive color associations that require minimal cognitive processing.

These visual frameworks transform abstract financial concepts into concrete, manageable elements that can be quickly assessed and adjusted without the mental fatigue that traditional spreadsheet-based systems often create for neurodivergent minds.

Icon-based tracking systems leverage symbol recognition to create instant comprehension of financial categories and progress, reducing the cognitive load required for financial monitoring while increasing engagement through visually appealing and memorable representations.

Money Map Creation

Visual flow charts that illustrate income sources flowing toward specific goals create clear understanding of financial priorities while making abstract concepts like budgeting and saving feel concrete and achievable through spatial representation.

Dashboard designs using tools like Notion, Tiller, or even analog whiteboards provide at-a-glance financial status updates without requiring deep dives into complex data that might overwhelm or confuse during routine financial check-ins.

Progress visualization through charts, graphs, and visual indicators transforms incremental financial improvements into motivating feedback that celebrates small wins while maintaining focus on long-term objectives through continuous positive reinforcement.

Micro-Actions for Building Momentum

Two-minute financial rituals break overwhelming tasks into manageable actions that can be completed without significant mental preparation or energy expenditure, creating consistent progress through small, sustainable steps that build confidence over time.

These micro-actions work by leveraging the brain's natural tendency to seek completion and accomplishment, providing frequent opportunities for success that build positive associations with financial management rather than avoidance patterns.

Gamification elements including timers, point systems, and achievement tracking transform routine financial tasks into engaging activities that provide immediate feedback and reward, making wealth-building feel more like play than work.

Implementation Framework

Daily balance checks that take less than thirty seconds create awareness without overwhelm while building familiarity with financial status that prevents small issues from becoming major problems through regular monitoring.

Five-dollar transfer rituals that move small amounts toward savings goals create momentum while demonstrating that wealth-building doesn't require large actions to produce meaningful results over time through consistent application.

Single expense logging exercises that record one daily purchase build awareness of spending patterns while developing financial mindfulness that improves decision-making through increased consciousness of money flow.

Habit Stacking for Sustainable Systems

Pairing financial tasks with established routines leverages existing neural pathways to create automatic behaviors that require minimal willpower or conscious decision-making, ensuring consistency through integration with daily life patterns.

This approach recognizes that creating entirely new habits requires significant mental energy, while attaching financial actions to existing routines allows them to benefit from already-established behavioral momentum.

Anchor habits that connect financial actions to specific triggers create reliable systems that function independently of mood or motivation, building wealth through consistent action regardless of daily energy levels or emotional states.

Strategic Habit Integration

Morning routine integration that includes financial check-ins after coffee or breakfast creates natural timing that feels organic rather than forced while ensuring financial awareness starts each day with positive intention.

Evening reflection practices that review financial progress during bedtime routines provide closure while reinforcing positive financial behaviors through acknowledgment and appreciation of daily wealth-building actions.

Transition ritual development that uses financial micro-actions as bridges between different activities creates multiple opportunities for wealth-building throughout the day while making financial management feel integrated into life rather than separate from it.

Tools for Executive Function & Emotional Regulation: Supporting Your Success

Executive function challenges common in neurodivergent individuals can create significant barriers to traditional financial management, making automation and supportive tools essential components of sustainable wealth-building systems rather than optional conveniences.

Understanding these challenges as neurological differences rather than personal failures enables strategic tool selection that compensates for executive function variations while amplifying existing strengths through thoughtful system design and implementation.

Emotional regulation support becomes equally important, as financial stress can trigger intense responses that interfere with rational decision-making, making emotional management tools crucial components of comprehensive financial wellness approaches.

Executive Function Support Systems

Automation of recurring financial tasks eliminates decision fatigue while ensuring critical actions occur consistently without requiring conscious memory or daily decision-making that might be compromised during challenging periods.

This systematic approach recognizes that executive function can vary significantly day to day, making automated systems essential for maintaining financial progress during periods of reduced cognitive availability or increased stress.

Tool selection should prioritize clean interfaces and minimal cognitive load, choosing platforms that present information clearly without overwhelming visual complexity that might interfere with quick decision-making or routine financial management.

Automation Strategy Development

Bill automation ensures timely payments while preventing late fees and credit damage that might result from forgotten due dates during periods of executive function challenges or life transitions.

Savings automation creates wealth-building momentum without requiring daily decisions while ensuring progress continues even during periods when financial management feels overwhelming or secondary to other pressing concerns.

Investment automation through dollar-cost averaging eliminates timing decisions while building long-term wealth through consistent market participation that doesn't depend on perfect market timing or continuous active management.

Clean Interface Technology

Platform selection should emphasize user experience design that reduces cognitive load through intuitive navigation and clear visual hierarchy that makes financial information accessible without overwhelming complexity or confusing layouts.

Apps like Monarch, Copilot Money, or YNAB provide financial management functionality with thoughtful design that accommodates diverse cognitive processing styles while maintaining powerful features that support sophisticated wealth-building strategies.

Reminder systems that provide gentle prompts without creating anxiety help maintain financial routines while respecting individual preferences for notification timing and intensity that support rather than stress daily life management.

User Experience Optimization

Interface customization enables personalization that accommodates individual visual processing preferences while maintaining functionality that supports comprehensive financial management without unnecessary complexity or feature overload.

Notification management allows control over reminder frequency and timing while ensuring important financial tasks receive attention without creating overwhelming digital noise that might interfere with focus or emotional regulation.

Data presentation options that include visual, numerical, and narrative formats enable information access through preferred learning channels while ensuring comprehensive understanding regardless of dominant processing style.

Emotional Regulation Strategies

Money mood tracking creates awareness of emotional patterns around financial activities while providing data that can guide timing and approach for financial tasks based on optimal emotional states for productive engagement.

This awareness enables strategic scheduling of financial activities during emotionally supportive periods while avoiding financial decision-making during vulnerable states that might lead to impulsive or counterproductive choices.

Grounding rituals that prepare the nervous system for financial activities create emotional safety while building positive associations with wealth-building actions through consistent self-care integration.

Emotional Support Implementation

Pre-financial breathwork that calms the nervous system before reviewing accounts or making financial decisions creates optimal mental states while preventing anxiety from interfering with rational assessment and strategic thinking.

Financial safe space creation through specific environments, music, or scents that promote calm and focus enables productive financial work while associating wealth-building activities with comfort and security rather than stress and overwhelm.

Post-financial celebration rituals that acknowledge completion of financial tasks build positive reinforcement while creating emotional rewards that encourage continued engagement with wealth-building activities through consistent positive associations.

Impulse Control Scaffolding

Structured systems that create friction around impulsive purchases provide time for reflection while maintaining access to desired items through delayed gratification approaches that honor both immediate desires and long-term financial goals.

Twenty-four-hour waiting periods for non-essential purchases allow emotional intensity to subside while providing opportunity for rational evaluation that considers financial impact alongside immediate satisfaction.

Wishlist systems that capture desired items without immediate purchase create satisfaction through acquisition planning while providing alternatives to impulsive buying that might compromise financial progress or create regret.

Impulse Management Tools

Prepaid card systems that limit available spending create natural boundaries while preventing overspending without requiring constant vigilance or willpower that might be compromised during stressful periods or executive function challenges.

Cash envelope methods that allocate specific amounts for discretionary spending provide physical limitations while creating tangible awareness of spending limits that support mindful consumption rather than unconscious purchasing patterns.

Future self visualization exercises that consider long-term impact of current financial choices build decision-making frameworks while connecting immediate actions to future consequences on structured reflection processes.

Neurodivergent Wealth Identity: Embracing Your Financial Superpowers

Traditional financial education often assumes neurotypical processing patterns, creating systems that feel foreign or overwhelming to neurodivergent minds while ignoring the unique strengths and perspectives that can create extraordinary wealth-building advantages.

Reframing neurodivergence as cognitive diversity rather than deficit enables recognition of special abilities that, when properly supported and channeled, can create innovative approaches to wealth building that surpass conventional methods through creative problem-solving and systematic thinking.

This identity shift transforms perceived limitations into recognized superpowers while building confidence and self-advocacy that supports long-term financial success through authentic self-expression and strategic strength utilization.

Reframing Financial Success

Success metrics that honor neurodivergent values might prioritize consistency over perfection, progress over performance, and system sustainability over conventional benchmarks that don't account for diverse cognitive processing styles and life management approaches.

Your financial system should feel supportive rather than punitive, providing structure that enhances rather than restricts your natural capabilities while accommodating the unique rhythms and patterns that characterize your optimal functioning.

Sovereignty-focused wealth building emphasizes independence and self-determination rather than external validation, creating financial security that enables authentic self-expression and life choices that align with individual values and preferences.

Success Redefinition Framework

Personal progress markers that celebrate incremental improvements build motivation while recognizing that sustainable change occurs through consistent small actions rather than dramatic transformations that might be unsustainably long-term.

System effectiveness measures focus on how well financial tools support daily life rather than absolute performance numbers, prioritizing functionality that enhances well-being over arbitrary benchmarks that might not reflect individual success.

Authenticity integration ensures that wealth-building approaches align with personal values and cognitive style rather than forcing adaptation to systems that feel unnatural or unsustainable for long-term implementation and success.

Mythic Identity for Neurodivergent Creators

Your neurodivergent brain represents unique coding that provides special abilities in pattern recognition, systematic thinking, creative problem-solving, and innovative approaches that can create significant advantages in wealth building when properly understood and applied.

This mythic identity positions neurodivergence as powerful differentiation rather than limitation, recognizing that diverse cognitive approaches often identify opportunities and solutions that neurotypical perspectives might overlook through conventional thinking patterns.

Financial systems designed for neurodivergent minds become armor that protects and empowers rather than cages that restrict, providing structure that enhances natural abilities while compensating for areas that need additional support.

Mythic Identity Development

Superpower recognition involves identifying specific neurodivergent strengths that provide wealth-building advantages, such as attention to detail, pattern recognition, systematic thinking, or creative problem-solving that can be strategically applied to financial success.

Strength-based system design creates financial approaches that leverage natural abilities while providing support for challenging areas, ensuring that wealth-building feels aligned with rather than opposed to cognitive style and personal preferences.

Narrative transformation shifts from deficit-focused language to strength-based identity that celebrates cognitive diversity while building confidence in unique approaches to financial success and wealth creation.

Sacred Financial Practices

Ritualization of financial activities transforms routine tasks into meaningful practices that honor your commitment to financial sovereignty while creating emotional connection to wealth-building activities through intentional ceremony and appreciation.

These sacred practices recognize that neurodivergent minds often benefit from routine and ritual that provide structure and meaning while reducing anxiety through predictable patterns that create safety and confidence.

Personal financial ceremonies might include specific timing, location, music, or preparation that makes financial work feel special and important rather than tedious or overwhelming, building positive associations through thoughtful environmental design.

Sacred Practice Implementation

Monthly financial ceremonies that review progress and set intentions create meaningful connection to wealth-building while providing regular opportunity for celebration and course correction through structured reflection and planning.

Daily financial gratitude practices that acknowledge progress and resources build positive mindset while reinforcing abundance thinking that supports continued wealth-building through optimistic and appreciative perspective.

Seasonal financial planning rituals that align with natural cycles provide structure while honoring the cyclical nature of motivation and energy that characterizes many neurodivergent experiences of productivity and focus.

Supportive Technology Integration

Technology selection for neurodivergent wealth building should prioritize accessibility, customization, and cognitive load reduction while providing powerful functionality that supports sophisticated financial management without overwhelming complexity or confusing interfaces.

These tools become extensions of cognitive ability rather than sources of frustration, amplifying natural strengths while providing compensation for executive function challenges through thoughtful design and strategic implementation.

Integration strategies should consider sensory preferences, attention patterns, and processing styles while ensuring technology supports rather than hinders financial progress through user-centered design and personalized configuration.

Accessible Financial Apps

Visual-first applications that present information through charts, graphs, and icons rather than dense numerical data create immediate understanding while reducing cognitive processing time required for financial assessment and decision-making.

Customizable interfaces that allow adjustment of colors, layouts, and information density accommodate individual sensory preferences while ensuring financial tools feel comfortable and supportive rather than overwhelming or stressful.

Gamification features that provide points, achievements, and progress tracking transform financial management into engaging activities while providing frequent positive reinforcement that builds motivation and consistency.

App Selection Criteria

User interface simplicity that avoids cluttered designs and confusing navigation enables focus on financial goals rather than technology frustration while ensuring accessibility for diverse cognitive processing styles and attention patterns.

Automation capabilities that reduce required daily decisions support executive function while ensuring financial progress continues during periods of reduced capacity or increased stress that might interfere with routine management.

Integration options that connect with existing tools and workflows prevent system fragmentation while ensuring comprehensive financial management without requiring multiple platform management that might become overwhelming.

Digital Organization Systems

Cloud-based organization that provides access across devices ensures financial information remains available without location restrictions while providing backup protection against device failure or loss that might compromise financial records.

Template systems that provide pre-built structures for budgeting, tracking, and planning reduce setup time while ensuring comprehensive coverage of financial areas that might otherwise be overlooked during initial system development.

Collaborative features that enable trusted support person access provide assistance during challenging periods while maintaining primary control over financial decisions and privacy preferences that honor individual autonomy.

Organization Strategy Development

File naming conventions that create intuitive organization enable quick information retrieval while preventing lost documents or confusion that might interfere with efficient financial management and record-keeping.

Backup systems that protect financial data through automatic cloud storage prevent loss while ensuring business continuity during technology failures or transitions that might otherwise disrupt financial management systems.

Update schedules that maintain current information without requiring daily attention ensure accuracy while preventing overwhelming maintenance tasks that might discourage continued system use and development.

Your Neurodivergent Wealth Action Plan

Building adaptive wealth systems requires understanding your unique cognitive profile while systematically implementing tools and strategies that support long-term financial success through personalized approaches that honor your neurological authenticity.

This action plan recognizes that implementation may require experimentation and adjustment as you discover which approaches work best for your individual brain while maintaining flexibility to adapt systems as needs change and understanding develops.

Success comes through consistent application of supportive systems rather than perfect execution, emphasizing progress over perfection while building confidence through accumulated positive experiences with financial management and wealth creation.

Assessment and Foundation Phase (Month 1)

Cognitive Profile Understanding

Complete honest assessment of your executive function strengths and challenges while identifying specific areas where additional support would improve financial management effectiveness and reduce stress or overwhelm.

Identify sensory preferences and processing styles that affect your interaction with financial information while determining optimal environments and tools that support focused and productive financial work.

Document current financial challenges and successes while establishing baseline understanding that guides system development and enables progress measurement through objective assessment of improvement areas.

Initial System Development

Select primary financial management tool based on cognitive fit rather than features alone while prioritizing user experience that feels intuitive and supportive rather than frustrating or overwhelming.

Establish basic automation for essential functions including bill payments and savings transfers while reducing daily financial decisions that require executive function and might be compromised during challenging periods.

Create visual tracking system for one primary financial goal while building positive experience with adaptive financial management that can be expanded as confidence and competence develop.

System Refinement Phase (Month 2-3)

Habit Integration Development

Identify three existing daily routines where financial micro-actions can be attached while leveraging established behavioral patterns that require minimal willpower to maintain consistently over time.

Develop morning and evening financial rituals that feel natural and supportive while creating structured opportunities for financial awareness and progress without overwhelming daily routines.

Implement visual progress tracking that provides immediate feedback while building motivation through visible evidence of wealth-building success that reinforces continued engagement with financial goals.

Emotional Support Integration

Create personal financial safe space that supports calm and focused financial work while associating wealth-building activities with comfort and security rather than stress and anxiety.

Develop pre-financial work rituals that prepare mind and body for productive financial activities while building positive associations that encourage consistent engagement rather than avoidance patterns.

Establish celebration practices that acknowledge financial achievements while building positive reinforcement that supports continued wealth-building through recognition of progress and success.

Expansion and Mastery Phase (Month 4-6)

Advanced System Development

Expand automation systems to include investment contributions and goal-based savings while building wealth-building momentum that operates independently of daily decision-making and executive function availability.

Develop comprehensive visual dashboard that provides at-a-glance financial status while integrating all major financial areas into unified system that supports strategic decision-making without information overwhelm.

Create quarterly review systems that assess progress and adjust strategies while maintaining long-term perspective that honors both achievement and areas for continued development and improvement.

Community and Support Integration

Identify supportive community resources that understand neurodivergent financial needs while building network of understanding and encouragement that supports continued growth and development.

Develop mentorship or coaching relationships with financial professionals who understand neurodivergent learning styles while ensuring expert guidance that honors cognitive diversity and individual needs.

Create sharing and teaching opportunities that reinforce learning while contributing to neurodivergent financial education through community support and knowledge sharing that benefits others.

Long-term Sustainability Phase (Month 7+)

System Optimization and Evolution

Regularly assess and refine systems based on changing needs and understanding while maintaining flexibility that accommodates life transitions and evolving financial goals that require system adaptation.

Develop advanced strategies that leverage neurodivergent strengths in pattern recognition and systematic thinking while building sophisticated wealth-building approaches that maximize cognitive advantages.

Create legacy planning that ensures financial systems and knowledge transfer to support family and community while building generational wealth that honors neurodivergent strengths and perspectives.

Community Leadership Development

Share successful strategies with other neurodivergent individuals while building expertise that supports community wealth-building through education and encouragement that validates diverse approaches to financial success.

Develop training and mentorship skills that enable teaching of adaptive financial systems while building income opportunities through specialized knowledge that serves underserved neurodivergent community.

Advocate for inclusive financial education that recognizes cognitive diversity while working to change systems that exclude or disadvantage neurodivergent individuals through discrimination or inappropriate design.

The Sovereignty of Difference

As we conclude this empowering exploration of adaptive wealth systems, remember that your neurodivergent mind possesses unique gifts that, when properly supported through thoughtful system design, can create extraordinary financial success that honors your authentic self while building lasting prosperity.

The strategies we have explored together demonstrate that financial success doesn't require conformity to neurotypical norms but rather the courage to design systems that work with your brain rather than against it, transforming perceived challenges into recognized superpowers.

Your commitment to building wealth through adaptive systems positions you as pioneer in inclusive financial education while demonstrating that cognitive diversity represents strength rather than limitation when approached with understanding and strategic support.

The wealth you build through neurodivergent-friendly systems creates ripple effects that inspire others while challenging conventional approaches that fail to recognize the value and potential of diverse cognitive styles in financial success and wealth creation.

Your sovereignty lies not in changing yourself to fit existing systems but in creating systems that celebrate and amplify your unique cognitive gifts while building financial security that enables authentic self-expression and life choices aligned with your values.

Affirmation for Neurodivergent Sovereignty:

"I build wealth in my own rhythm."

"My systems are sacred. My rituals are real."

"I honor my wiring, protect my peace, and rise without apology."

Your journey toward financial sovereignty begins with the next adaptive system you implement, the next micro-action you complete, the next moment you choose to honor your neurodivergent strengths rather than apologize for your cognitive differences. In this way, every financial decision becomes an act of self-advocacy and authentic power that builds not just wealth but also the confidence to thrive as exactly who you are.

The revolution starts now. Your neurodivergent wealth awaits your commitment to building systems that celebrate rather than constrain your magnificent, uniquely wired mind.

Chapter 11: Navigating Financial Abuse or Control—The Liberation Ledger

"Your financial freedom is not a privilege to be granted by another—it is your birthright to be reclaimed. In the shadows of control and manipulation, you hold within yourself the power to break every chain, to reclaim every dollar of your dignity, and to build a fortress of independence that no one can breach."

Welcome, dear survivor, to a sanctuary of understanding where your experience is honored, your strength is recognized, and your path to liberation is illuminated with both compassion and concrete action. Here, within these carefully crafted pages, we embark upon a journey that acknowledges the profound courage it takes to recognize financial abuse while providing you with the tools, resources, and unwavering support necessary to reclaim your economic sovereignty.

As we venture together into this empowering exploration, I invite you to know that you are not alone in this struggle, nor are you responsible for the manipulation and control that has been inflicted upon you. Instead, embrace the profound truth that emerges from these teachings: your recognition of financial abuse represents the first powerful step toward freedom, and your commitment to liberation demonstrates a strength that no abuser can diminish or destroy.

This chapter serves as your comprehensive guide through the complex landscape of financial abuse recovery, providing both emotional support and tactical strategies that honor the delicate balance between safety and action. Together, we will explore how to identify the subtle and overt signs of financial control, develop secure exit strategies that protect your wellbeing, and rebuild your financial life with the wisdom and strength that comes from surviving and thriving beyond abuse.

Spotting Manipulation & Reclaiming Autonomy: Recognizing the Invisible Chains

Financial abuse operates through a sophisticated web of control that often masquerades as care, protection, or partnership, making it particularly insidious because it corrupts the very foundation of trust that healthy relationships require while systematically dismantling your economic independence and self-determination.

Understanding the patterns of financial manipulation enables you to distinguish between genuine support and coercive control, empowering you to name what you are experiencing while building the emotional clarity necessary to take protective action on your own behalf.

This recognition process requires tremendous courage because it often means acknowledging painful truths about relationships and situations you may have hoped were different, while validating your instincts and experiences that others may have dismissed or minimized.

Red Flags of Financial Control: The Architecture of Economic Abuse

Financial control manifests through systematic restrictions on your access to money, resources, and financial decision-making power while creating dependency that makes leaving or asserting independence feel impossible or dangerous.

These restrictions often begin subtly through seemingly helpful offers to "manage" your finances or "protect" you from financial stress, gradually escalating into comprehensive control that monitors, restricts, and punishes your economic choices and autonomy.

Recognizing these patterns enables you to understand that what you are experiencing has a name, follows predictable patterns, and represents serious abuse that deserves intervention and support rather than endurance or accommodation.

Access Restrictions and Financial Isolation

Bank account control where you are denied access to your own accounts, prevented from having individual accounts, or required to obtain permission for withdrawals represents fundamental violation of your financial autonomy and legal rights.

Income interference including being prevented from working, having your paychecks controlled by someone else, or being sabotaged in educational or career pursuits creates economic dependence that serves the abuser's control while limiting your options for independence.

Credit and debt sabotage through unauthorized use of your identity for loans, credit cards, or financial obligations creates long-term financial damage while binding you to the abuser through shared financial liabilities that complicate escape planning.

Surveillance and Micromanagement

Spending monitoring that requires you to account for every purchase, provide receipts for all transactions, or justify normal living expenses creates an atmosphere of constant scrutiny that erodes your sense of privacy and autonomy.

Financial decision exclusion where major and minor financial choices are made without your input while you bear the consequences demonstrates the abuser's belief that you have no right to participate in decisions affecting your own economic wellbeing.

Resource rationing that provides barely adequate funds for necessities while withholding money for personal needs, emergencies, or reasonable wants maintains your vulnerability while demonstrating power through artificial scarcity.

Emotional Manipulation Tactics: The Psychology of Financial Control

Emotional manipulation accompanying financial abuse often involves reframing control as care while using guilt, shame, and fear to maintain compliance and prevent you from seeking help or asserting your rights.

These tactics exploit your natural desire for love and security while systematically undermining your confidence in your own judgment and capabilities, making resistance feel dangerous or impossible.

Understanding these psychological patterns helps you recognize that your emotional responses are normal reactions to abnormal treatment while building the internal strength necessary to resist manipulation and seek appropriate support.

Disguised Control and False Protection

"Helping" narratives that position financial control as protection from your own poor judgment or external threats mask the abuser's desire for power while making resistance appear ungrateful or irrational.

Competency attacks that consistently undermine your intelligence, decision-making ability, or financial knowledge create self-doubt while justifying increased control through manufactured evidence of your supposed incompetence.

Isolation from financial education or resources prevents you from developing knowledge and skills that would enable independence while maintaining the abuser's position as the sole financial authority in the relationship.

Guilt and Obligation Manipulation

Debt rhetoric that constantly reminds you of what you "owe" for housing, food, or other basic needs creates artificial obligation while ignoring the abuser's equally important responsibilities and your own contributions to the relationship.

Financial inadequacy messaging that consistently reinforces your supposed inability to manage money independently undermines your confidence while creating learned helplessness that serves the abuser's control agenda.

Consequence threats about what will happen if you assert independence or resist control create fear-based compliance while suggesting that the abuser's reaction to your autonomy would be your fault rather than their choice.

Reclaiming Autonomy: The First Steps Toward Freedom

Reclaiming financial autonomy requires careful planning that prioritizes your safety while systematically building resources and knowledge that will support your eventual independence from abusive control.

This process must balance the need for action with the reality that abusers often escalate control and violence when they sense their power is threatened, making strategic secrecy and gradual preparation essential for successful liberation.

Beginning this reclamation process represents profound courage and marks the start of your journey toward economic sovereignty and personal freedom that no one can take away from you.

Secret Resource Building

Freedom fund development through hidden savings accounts, cash reserves, or secure financial resources provides the foundation for independence while creating options that exist outside the abuser's knowledge or control.

This fund requires careful management to avoid detection while building sufficient resources to support immediate safety needs and transition expenses that will enable you to leave safely when ready.

Account establishment in your name only, preferably at financial institutions the abuser doesn't use, creates secure access to resources while beginning to rebuild your independent financial identity.

Knowledge as Resistance

Financial literacy development through discrete learning represents powerful resistance against control while building capabilities that will serve your independence and long-term security beyond the immediate crisis.

This education might occur through online resources, library materials, or trusted advisors who understand your situation while maintaining confidentiality about your learning and planning activities.

Documentation practices that secretly record financial abuse patterns create evidence while building your own understanding of the scope and impact of the control you are experiencing.

Strategic Documentation and Evidence

Abuse pattern recording through photos, written records, or audio documentation creates evidence while helping you recognize the full extent of control that you might have normalized or minimized.

Financial record preservation through copies of important documents stored in secure locations protects your access to vital information while preventing the abuser from controlling your identity documents or financial history.

Communication evidence that demonstrates financial threats, control, or manipulation provides documentation while supporting future legal action or intervention services that might be necessary for your protection.

Exit Strategies & Support Networks: Planning Your Path to Freedom

Escaping financial abuse requires comprehensive planning that addresses immediate safety concerns while building the resources and support systems necessary to maintain independence after leaving the abusive situation.

This planning process acknowledges that leaving often represents the most dangerous time in an abusive relationship while providing concrete steps to maximize your safety and success during this vulnerable transition period.

Professional support from experts trained in financial abuse provides specialized assistance while connecting you with resources and strategies that account for the unique challenges of economic manipulation and control.

Digital Escape Preparation: Securing Your Virtual Freedom

Digital security becomes critical when preparing to leave financial abuse because abusers often monitor electronic communications, banking activities, and online behavior as extensions of their control and surveillance systems.

This preparation involves both protecting your private activities while building secure communication channels and financial resources that exist outside the abuser's knowledge or access.

Technology tools that seem routine and innocent can provide powerful support for escape planning when used strategically while maintaining the appearance of normal activity that doesn't trigger suspicion or escalated control.

Document Security and Identity Protection

Personal document collection including identification, Social Security cards, birth certificates, and financial records requires secure storage outside the abuser's reach while ensuring quick access during emergency departure situations.

Digital copies stored in secure cloud accounts or with trusted contacts provide backup access while physical documents hidden in safe locations offer redundancy that protects against discovery or destruction.

Password security through independent email accounts and strong authentication prevents the abuser from accessing your private communications or monitoring your escape planning activities.

Financial Account Development

Separate banking relationships at institutions unfamiliar to the abuser create secure financial resources while establishing credit history and banking relationships that will support your independent life.

Two-factor authentication and security measures that use your personal devices rather than shared communications protect account access while preventing unauthorized monitoring or interference.

Gradual resource transfer through small, irregular amounts helps build escape funds while avoiding patterns that might trigger suspicion or investigation from controlling partners who monitor spending carefully.

Secure Communication Channels

Private email accounts accessed only from secure locations or devices enable communication with support services while maintaining confidentiality about your escape planning and resource building activities.

VPN services and incognito browsing modes provide additional privacy protection while researching resources, legal options, or support services that could assist with your transition to independence.

Trusted contact networks that understand your situation provide communication channels while offering assistance with planning, resources, or emergency support during critical transition periods.

Financial Triage: Assessing and Protecting Your Economic Position

Understanding the full scope of financial damage enables strategic planning while preventing further harm through credit monitoring and protective measures that limit the abuser's ongoing ability to create financial problems.

This assessment process requires honest evaluation of your financial position while connecting with professional support that understands the unique challenges created by financial abuse and manipulation.

Immediate protective measures create stability while longer-term recovery planning addresses the comprehensive rebuilding necessary to restore your financial health and independence.

Credit Protection and Damage Assessment

Credit report review through all three major bureaus identifies unauthorized accounts while documenting the scope of financial damage that might require dispute processes and legal intervention.

Credit freeze implementation prevents new accounts from being opened in your name while stopping ongoing identity theft or credit sabotage that might continue after you recognize the abuse.

Fraud alerts on existing accounts notify you of suspicious activity while creating legal documentation of financial abuse that might support future legal action or insurance claims.

Professional Financial Support

Nonprofit credit counseling provides expert assessment while offering free or low-cost services that understand the unique challenges faced by abuse survivors in rebuilding financial stability.

Legal aid services specializing in financial abuse offer professional support while connecting you with attorneys who understand the intersection of domestic violence and economic control.

Banking assistance through victim services helps navigate account closures, dispute processes, and new account establishment while providing advocacy with financial institutions that might not understand abuse dynamics.

Emergency Resource Access

Survivor grant programs through domestic violence organizations provide immediate financial assistance while connecting you with specialized services that understand the comprehensive needs of abuse survivors.

Government assistance programs including temporary financial support, housing assistance, and healthcare access provide safety net resources while you rebuild independent financial stability.

Community support networks including religious organizations, community centers, and mutual aid groups offer additional resources while building social connections that support your healing and independence.

Support Systems: Building Your Liberation Network

Recovery from financial abuse requires comprehensive support that addresses both practical needs and emotional healing while connecting you with others who understand the unique challenges of economic manipulation and control.

This support network should include professional services, peer connections, and community resources that provide different types of assistance throughout your journey from recognizing abuse to building independent, thriving financial life.

Building these connections requires courage and discernment while recognizing that support comes in many forms and that different types of help serve different stages of your recovery and empowerment process.

Professional Support Services

Domestic violence hotlines provide crisis intervention while connecting you with local resources and safety planning assistance that understands the dangerous dynamics of leaving abusive relationships.

Trauma-informed financial coaches offer specialized expertise while providing practical guidance that accounts for the emotional impact of financial abuse on your relationship with money and financial decision-making.

Therapeutic support through counselors experienced with domestic violence provides emotional healing while building psychological strength that supports your practical recovery efforts and long-term wellbeing.

Peer Support Communities

Online survivor communities provide connection while offering shared experiences and practical advice from others who have successfully navigated similar challenges and rebuilt their financial lives.

Local support groups create in-person connections while building relationships that provide ongoing encouragement and practical assistance during the challenging process of establishing independence.

Survivor mentorship programs connect you with others who have achieved stability while providing inspiration and concrete guidance about navigating specific challenges and building sustainable success.

Community Resource Networks

Faith community support through understanding religious organizations provides spiritual strength while often offering practical assistance including temporary housing, financial aid, and emotional support.

Professional network building connects you with career opportunities while providing income potential that supports your independence and builds confidence in your capabilities and value.

Chapter 12: Financial Literacy for Creatives & Freelancers—Beyond the Basics

"Your art is not a commodity to be undervalued, nor is your financial future a luxury to be deferred. In the sacred dance between creativity and commerce, you hold the power to honor both your artistic vision and your economic sovereignty, weaving prosperity into the very fabric of your creative legacy."

Connect your artistic passion with financial success. This chapter celebrates your creative gifts and offers a path to building lasting wealth, ensuring your art thrives for years to come.

As we venture together into this empowering realm, I invite you to release any limiting beliefs that creativity and financial success exist in opposition to one another. Instead, embrace the profound truth that emerges from these pages: your artistic talents represent not just expressions of beauty and meaning, but valuable assets capable of generating abundant prosperity when approached with strategic wisdom and authentic self-advocacy.

This chapter serves as your comprehensive guide to navigating the unique financial landscape of creative work while building the economic foundation that allows your artistic voice to flourish without compromise. Together, we will explore how to price your worth with confidence, structure your business for long-term success, and create multiple income streams that provide both stability and creative freedom throughout your artistic journey.

Emotional Economics of Creative Work: Honoring Value Without Compromise

The intersection of creativity and commerce often becomes a battleground where artists struggle to balance authentic expression with financial necessity, creating internal conflicts that undermine both artistic integrity and economic prosperity when approached without clear boundaries and strategic thinking.

Understanding the emotional landscape of creative pricing requires recognizing that your artistic worth extends far beyond the materials and time invested in individual projects to encompass years of skill development, unique perspective, and the intangible value that only your creative vision can provide to clients and audiences.

This foundation enables confident pricing that honors both your artistic development and your financial needs while creating sustainable business practices that support long-term creative careers rather than the feast-or-famine cycles that plague many artists who undervalue their contributions to the world.

Pricing Your Worth Without Shame

The shame surrounding creative pricing often stems from societal messaging that artistic pursuits should be driven by passion rather than profit, creating false dichotomies that force artists to choose between financial success and creative authenticity when both can coexist harmoniously through strategic approach.

Detaching self-worth from pricing requires understanding that professional rates reflect the market value of your skills and experience rather than your intrinsic worth as a human being, enabling objective pricing decisions that serve both your business sustainability and your artistic development.

This separation allows for strategic pricing adjustments based on market conditions, project scope, and business objectives without triggering emotional responses that might lead to undercharging or defensive behaviors that damage client relationships and professional reputation.

Establishing Your Value Foundation

Market research provides objective framework for pricing decisions by analyzing what comparable creatives charge for similar work while considering factors like experience level, geographic location, and specialized skills that differentiate your offerings from standard market rates.

Skill inventory documentation helps quantify the expertise you bring to projects beyond basic creative execution, including technical proficiency, industry knowledge, project management abilities, and unique perspectives that add value for clients and justify premium pricing.

Cost analysis including both direct expenses and overhead requirements ensures pricing covers business sustainability while providing fair compensation for your time and expertise that enables continued professional development and creative growth.

Strategic Pricing Models: Sliding Scale vs. Premium

Sliding scale pricing serves specific strategic purposes including community building, skill development projects, and mission-aligned work while requiring clear criteria and boundaries that prevent exploitation and maintain business sustainability over time.

Premium pricing positions you as a specialist while attracting clients who value quality and expertise over low costs, creating relationships with stakeholders who appreciate your artistic vision and are willing to invest appropriately in exceptional creative work.

The key lies in intentional application of each model rather than defaulting to lower prices out of fear or uncertainty, ensuring that pricing decisions align with business objectives and artistic goals rather than external pressures or internal insecurities.

Implementation Strategies

Client categorization based on project type, budget capacity, and alignment with your artistic mission enables strategic pricing that balances financial sustainability with opportunities for meaningful creative work and community contribution.

Value-based pricing focuses on client outcomes rather than time invested, allowing premium rates for projects where your creative expertise generates significant value while providing flexibility for time-efficient execution of high-impact work.

Package development creates clear pricing structures that simplify decision-making for both artist and client while establishing boundaries around scope creep and additional requests that might otherwise compromise project profitability.

Emotional Boundaries Around Discounts and Exposure

Professional boundary setting protects both your financial interests and creative energy by establishing clear policies around discount requests, exposure opportunities, and friend rates that maintain business sustainability while preserving personal relationships.

The exposure economy often exploits creative professionals by promising future opportunities in exchange for current unpaid work, requiring careful evaluation of actual potential benefits versus immediate financial sacrifice and opportunity costs.

Friend rates require particular attention because personal relationships can complicate professional boundaries, making it essential to develop clear policies that honor friendships while maintaining business integrity and financial sustainability.

Boundary Development Framework

Exposure evaluation criteria help assess whether unpaid opportunities provide genuine value through skill development, portfolio enhancement, or networking benefits that justify the financial sacrifice and time investment required.

Discount policies establish clear parameters for when and how much to reduce standard rates while maintaining professional credibility and business sustainability that prevents the race-to-the-bottom pricing that destroys creative industries.

Relationship preservation strategies enable maintenance of personal connections while upholding professional standards through clear communication about business requirements and alternative ways to support friends without compromising financial boundaries.

Financial Stress and Creative Flow

Financial instability creates mental and emotional barriers that directly impact creative performance by triggering stress responses that interfere with the relaxed, open mindset necessary for innovative thinking and artistic expression.

The connection between financial security and creative freedom becomes evident when artists with stable income streams demonstrate greater willingness to take creative risks and explore innovative approaches that might not have immediate commercial appeal.

Understanding this relationship enables strategic financial planning that prioritizes economic stability as a foundation for artistic development rather than viewing financial concerns as separate from or opposed to creative goals and artistic integrity.

Stress Reduction Through Financial Planning

Emergency fund development specifically for creative professionals should account for irregular income patterns while providing buffer for creative exploration periods and economic downturns that might otherwise force compromising artistic vision for immediate income.

Income diversification reduces dependency on individual clients or projects while creating multiple revenue streams that provide stability during client transitions or seasonal fluctuations in creative industry demand.

Financial tracking and budgeting systems designed for irregular income help manage cash flow volatility while providing clear picture of business performance that enables informed decision-making about pricing, expenses, and investment priorities.

Tactical Money Moves for Freelancers: Professional Financial Management

Successful creative freelancing requires systematic approaches to financial management that address the unique challenges of irregular income, client payment issues, and business expense tracking while maintaining professional credibility and legal compliance.

These tactical strategies transform chaotic financial management into streamlined systems that support business growth while providing the documentation and organization necessary for tax compliance and strategic financial planning.

Implementation of professional financial practices positions creative freelancers as serious business professionals while creating foundations for sustainable growth and long-term wealth building that extends beyond project-based income.

Invoicing with Authority

Professional invoicing establishes credibility while protecting cash flow through clear terms, systematic processes, and consistent follow-up that reduces payment delays and establishes expectations for professional business relationships.

Invoice design and content should reflect your brand while including all necessary information for prompt payment including detailed scope descriptions, payment terms, late fee policies, and contact information that facilitates smooth transaction processing.

Automated systems reduce administrative burden while ensuring consistent communication that maintains professional relationships during payment discussions and prevents small issues from becoming major conflicts that damage client relationships.

Professional Invoicing Systems

Platform selection between services like Wave, HoneyBook, or Bonsai should consider features including automated reminders, payment processing integration, expense tracking capabilities, and client portal functionality that streamlines business operations.

Payment terms establishment including net-30 or net-15 schedules, accepted payment methods, and late fee structures should be clearly communicated before project commencement while being consistently applied across all client relationships.

Follow-up protocols for overdue payments should maintain professional tone while applying appropriate pressure that encourages payment without damaging relationships or creating unnecessary conflicts that might affect future opportunities.

Contract Development and Intellectual Property Protection

Well-crafted contracts protect both creative work and financial interests by establishing clear scope boundaries, payment schedules, intellectual property ownership, and revision policies that prevent scope creep and ensure appropriate compensation.

Copyright understanding enables strategic decisions about intellectual property retention while creating opportunities for ongoing licensing revenue that extends value beyond initial project completion.

Kill fee and revision policies protect time investment while establishing boundaries around client changes that might otherwise compromise project profitability or creative integrity through excessive revision cycles.

Contract Essentials

Scope definition should be detailed enough to prevent misunderstandings while providing flexibility for creative evolution that serves project objectives without opening unlimited revision possibilities that destroy profitability.

Payment schedule structuring through milestone-based payments or percentage deposits reduces financial risk while improving cash flow management that enables better business planning and reduces collection challenges.

Intellectual property clauses should clearly define ownership rights, usage limitations, and future licensing opportunities while protecting both immediate compensation and long-term revenue potential from creative work.

Business and Personal Finance Separation

Business entity establishment through LLC formation or other structures provides legal protection while enabling professional banking relationships and simplified tax preparation that supports long-term business development and wealth building.

Separate banking accounts prevent commingling of personal and business funds while simplifying bookkeeping and tax preparation that reduces accounting costs and ensures compliance with business regulations and tax requirements.

Business credit development creates opportunities for equipment financing and business expansion while building financial track record that supports future investment opportunities and professional credibility.

Financial System Development

Bookkeeping systems using QuickBooks, Xero, or custom spreadsheet templates should track income sources, business expenses, and project profitability while providing reports that inform pricing decisions and business development strategies.

Monthly financial reviews create accountability while identifying trends in income, expenses, and profitability that inform strategic decisions about pricing, marketing focus, and business development priorities.

Tax preparation organization through systematic record-keeping reduces accounting fees while ensuring compliance with tax regulations and maximum deduction utilization that optimizes after-tax income and business profitability.

Tax Strategy for Irregular Income

Creative professionals face unique tax challenges including irregular income patterns, diverse expense categories, and business structure decisions that require strategic planning to optimize tax efficiency and cash flow management.

Quarterly tax payment systems help manage cash flow while preventing large year-end tax obligations that might strain business finances during slow periods or economic downturns that affect creative industry demand.

Deduction maximization through systematic expense tracking includes equipment, software, studio space, professional development, and even research materials that support creative work while reducing taxable income through legitimate business expenses.

Business Structure Optimization

Sole proprietorship provides simplicity while LLC formation offers liability protection and potential tax advantages that justify additional administrative requirements for growing creative businesses.

S-Corporation election might provide tax benefits for higher-earning creatives through salary and distribution optimization while requiring additional administrative compliance that should be evaluated based on income levels and long-term business goals.

Professional consultation with tax advisors familiar with creative industries ensures optimal structure selection while maintaining compliance with changing tax regulations that affect freelance and creative business taxation.

Creative Asset Building: Monetizing Your Artistic Legacy

Creative professionals possess unique opportunities to build wealth through intellectual property development, brand building, and passive income creation that extends value far beyond traditional service-based business models.

These asset-building strategies create ongoing revenue streams while preserving and monetizing creative work through licensing, digital products, and brand development that compound over time into substantial wealth accumulation.

Understanding and implementing these approaches transforms creative work from time-based income into asset-based wealth building that provides increasing financial freedom and creative autonomy throughout your artistic career.

Licensing and Intellectual Property Monetization

Creative work licensing enables ongoing revenue generation from existing artistic output through strategic partnerships with brands, publishers, and manufacturers who utilize your creative assets in commercial applications.

Copyright protection and registration provide legal foundation for licensing while establishing clear ownership rights that enable confident negotiation with potential licensees who seek to utilize your creative work.

Platform development through Creative Market, Gumroad, or Ko-fi creates direct sales channels while building audience relationships that support ongoing product development and marketing through engaged customer communities.

Licensing Strategy Development

Portfolio development for licensing should consider commercial applications while maintaining artistic integrity through strategic creation of work that appeals to licensing partners without compromising creative vision.

Pricing structures for licensing should account for usage scope, exclusivity requirements, and duration while ensuring appropriate compensation for both immediate licensing fees and ongoing royalty payments.

Partnership development with brands and manufacturers creates opportunities for larger licensing deals while building industry relationships that support ongoing business development and creative project opportunities.

Income Stream Diversification

Multiple revenue sources reduce financial risk while creating stability that enables creative exploration and artistic development without constant pressure for immediate commercial success from every creative project.

Teaching opportunities through workshops, online courses, or educational content creation leverage existing expertise while building authority and additional income streams that complement primary creative work.

Product development including merchandise, digital downloads, or physical products extends brand reach while creating passive income opportunities that generate revenue without direct time investment for each sale.

Diversification Implementation

Community-supported models like Patreon or Substack create predictable income through subscription-based fan support while building engaged audiences that provide feedback and marketing support for creative projects.

Affiliate marketing through product recommendations relevant to your creative niche generates commission income while providing value to audiences through curated product suggestions that align with their interests and needs.

Brand partnership development creates sponsored content opportunities while maintaining authentic voice through strategic selection of partnerships that align with artistic values and audience interests.

Retirement Planning for Creative Careers

Creative professionals without traditional employer benefits must proactively plan for retirement through individual account development and investment strategies that accommodate irregular income patterns.

Solo 401(k) accounts enable significant tax-deferred contributions while providing loan options and investment flexibility that traditional employer plans might not offer to self-employed creative professionals.

SEP IRA and Simple IRA options provide alternatives for creative businesses with employees while offering substantial contribution limits that enable accelerated retirement savings during high-income periods.

Retirement Strategy Implementation

Contribution timing should account for irregular income while maximizing tax advantages through strategic timing of contributions during high-income periods that optimize tax deduction benefits.

Investment selection within retirement accounts should consider long-term growth potential while maintaining appropriate risk levels for different life stages and financial goals that support creative career longevity.

Backup planning for creative professionals should include disability insurance and career transition strategies that protect retirement savings during periods of reduced earning capacity or industry changes.

Mindset Shifts for Financial Sovereignty: Rewriting Creative Narratives

The transformation from struggling artist to financially sovereign creative requires fundamental shifts in thinking about money, success, and the relationship between artistic integrity and financial prosperity that enables sustainable creative careers.

These mindset changes challenge cultural narratives that romanticize artistic poverty while embracing wealth building as creative act that enables greater artistic freedom and community contribution through financial resources and economic independence.

Integration of these perspectives creates foundation for strategic decision-making that honors both artistic values and financial goals while building sustainable creative careers that support long-term artistic development and community contribution.

From Starving Artist to Strategic Creator

The starving artist myth damages creative communities by suggesting that financial struggle validates artistic authenticity while prosperity indicates creative compromise, creating false dichotomies that limit both artistic and financial development.

Strategic creators understand that financial stability enables greater creative risks and artistic exploration by removing survival pressure that might otherwise force compromising artistic vision for immediate income through commercial work.

This reframe positions wealth building as creative strategy that supports artistic development rather than opposing it, enabling long-term artistic careers that maintain creative integrity while building financial security.

Identity Transformation Process

Professional identity development includes both artistic vision and business acumen while recognizing that creative professionals must navigate commercial realities without sacrificing authentic creative expression or artistic integrity.

Success redefinition expands beyond artistic recognition to include financial sustainability, creative autonomy, and community impact that provides multiple measures of achievement and professional fulfillment.

Legacy thinking considers long-term artistic contribution while building financial resources that enable ongoing creative work and community support throughout extended creative careers that may span decades.

Building Wealth as Creative Rebellion

Wealth accumulation by creative professionals challenges systems that exploit artistic labor while building economic power that enables artistic independence and community investment through financial resources and strategic influence.

This approach recognizes financial success as form of resistance against exploitative industry practices while creating examples that inspire other creatives to demand fair compensation for their valuable contributions to culture and commerce.

Wealthy creatives become cultural influencers who can support emerging artists while funding artistic projects and community initiatives that might not otherwise receive adequate financial backing through traditional funding sources.

Rebellion Through Prosperity

Economic independence enables artistic risk-taking while providing security that allows exploration of experimental work or socially conscious projects that might not have immediate commercial viability.

Community investment through successful creative businesses creates employment opportunities while supporting local artistic communities through purchasing, partnerships, and mentorship that strengthens creative ecosystems.

Cultural influence through financial success provides platforms for advocating artistic value while challenging systemic undervaluation of creative work through demonstration that creative professionals can achieve substantial financial success.

Community Wealth Building for Creatives

Artist collectives and cooperative models create shared resources while building community wealth through collaborative approach that reduces individual financial burden while expanding opportunities through group purchasing power and shared expertise.

Co-working spaces and shared studios reduce overhead costs while building professional networks that generate referrals and collaboration opportunities that might not emerge through isolated individual practice.

Group investing and resource pooling enable access to equipment, education, and opportunities that might be unaffordable individually while building financial literacy and investment experience through collaborative learning and shared decision-making.

Community Implementation Strategies

Collective formation should establish clear governance structures while defining shared goals and individual responsibilities that prevent conflicts and ensure equitable benefit distribution among community members.

Resource sharing agreements require clear terms regarding usage, maintenance, and cost allocation while building trust through transparent communication and fair contribution systems that serve all participants.

Educational initiatives within creative communities build financial literacy while sharing knowledge and strategies that benefit entire creative ecosystems through improved economic outcomes for individual artists and creative businesses.

Your Creative Financial Action Plan

Implementing comprehensive financial management for creative careers requires systematic approach that addresses immediate cash flow needs while building long-term wealth through strategic planning and consistent action aligned with artistic goals and values.

This action plan provides framework for transforming creative careers into sustainable businesses while maintaining artistic integrity and building financial security that supports long-term creative development and community contribution.

Remember that financial mastery, like artistic skill, develops through consistent practice and continuous learning that builds capability over time through experience and strategic implementation of proven principles and practices.

Foundation Phase (Months 1-3)

Business Structure Development

Establish separate business banking accounts while researching appropriate business structure options including LLC formation or sole proprietorship based on income levels and growth projections for creative business development.

Implement basic bookkeeping systems using software or spreadsheet templates while establishing monthly review routines that track income sources, business expenses, and project profitability for strategic decision-making.

Develop professional invoicing processes including clear payment terms, automated reminders, and standard contract templates that protect both creative work and financial interests through systematic business practices.

Pricing and Boundaries

Complete market research for creative services while establishing pricing structures that reflect skill level and market position while providing sustainable income for business operation and artistic development.

Establish clear policies regarding discounts, friend rates, and exposure opportunities while developing communication strategies that maintain relationships while protecting financial boundaries and business sustainability.

Create standard contract templates including scope definitions, payment schedules, and intellectual property clauses while consulting legal professionals for complex projects or ongoing client relationships.

Growth Phase (Months 4-9)

Income Diversification

Develop multiple income streams including teaching, licensing, or product sales while building passive income opportunities that complement primary creative services without overwhelming creative capacity or compromising quality.

Build audience through content creation and community engagement while developing email lists and social media presence that supports marketing efforts and client development for sustainable business growth.

Investigate licensing opportunities for existing creative work while developing new work specifically for commercial licensing that provides ongoing revenue beyond initial creation investment.

Financial Optimization

Implement quarterly tax payment systems while maximizing business deductions through systematic expense tracking and professional tax consultation that optimizes tax efficiency and cash flow management.

Develop emergency fund specifically sized for creative business irregularities while implementing cash flow management systems that smooth income volatility through strategic savings and spending timing.

Begin retirement planning through appropriate account selection and regular contributions that account for irregular income while taking advantage of tax-deferred growth opportunities available to self-employed professionals.

Mastery Phase (Months 10+)

Wealth Building Integration

Develop investment strategy that complements creative career while building long-term wealth through diversified portfolio that provides financial security without requiring active management that might interfere with creative work.

Create legacy planning including intellectual property management and estate planning while building systems that protect creative assets and provide ongoing income for family or chosen beneficiaries.

Establish community investment and mentorship programs while sharing financial knowledge with other creatives through teaching or formal programs that strengthen creative communities through improved economic outcomes.

Advanced Strategy Implementation

Evaluate business structure optimization including S-Corporation election or other advanced strategies while working with qualified professionals to ensure tax efficiency and legal compliance as business income grows.

Develop sophisticated pricing strategies including value-based pricing and premium positioning while building reputation and client relationships that support higher rates and more selective project acceptance.

Build strategic partnerships and collaborative relationships while creating opportunities for larger projects and expanded market reach through professional networks and industry relationships that support continued business growth.

The Creative Wealth Revolution

As we conclude this empowering exploration of creative financial mastery, remember that you now possess the knowledge and tools necessary to build substantial wealth while honoring your artistic vision and maintaining creative integrity throughout your professional journey.

The strategies we have explored together demonstrate that creativity and commerce need not exist in opposition but can dance together in harmonious partnership that amplifies both artistic impact and financial prosperity through strategic thinking and professional implementation.

Your commitment to financial literacy as a creative professional positions you as part of a growing movement that challenges outdated narratives while building new models of creative success that inspire future generations of artists to pursue both artistic excellence and financial sovereignty.

The wealth you build through strategic creative practice creates ripple effects that extend far beyond personal benefit to strengthen entire creative communities while demonstrating that artistic work deserves fair compensation and professional respect that honors both creative contribution and economic value.

Your creative wealth rebellion begins with your next financial decision—whether it's raising your rates, diversifying your income, or starting that emergency fund. Each step toward financial sovereignty strengthens not just your own creative future but contributes to a cultural shift that values artistic work appropriately while building sustainable creative careers that can flourish for decades.

The revolution starts ***now***. Your art deserves prosperity, and prosperity deserves your art.

Chapter 13: Digital Security & Financial Privacy

"In this interconnected age of digital wealth, your financial privacy is not merely a preference—it is your fundamental right to sovereignty over your economic destiny. Every password you strengthen, every breach you prevent, and every digital boundary you establish becomes a declaration of independence from those who would exploit your financial vulnerabilities for their gain."

This is perhaps the most crucial chapter in your modern wealth rebellion journey—a sanctuary of knowledge designed to fortify your financial empire against the digital predators that lurk within our interconnected world. Here, within these meticulously crafted pages, we embark upon an essential exploration that transforms you from a vulnerable digital citizen into a fortress of financial security that cannot be easily breached or compromised.

As we venture together into this empowering realm of digital protection, I invite you to embrace this knowledge with the understanding that your financial security in the digital age requires the same strategic thinking and systematic approach that builds wealth itself. Every security measure you implement, every privacy boundary you establish, and every protective habit you develop becomes an investment in your long-term financial freedom and peace of mind.

This chapter serves as your comprehensive guide to mastering digital financial security, transforming complex cybersecurity concepts into accessible strategies that protect your wealth while enabling you to participate confidently in the digital economy. Together, we will explore the fundamental principles of digital wallet protection, develop robust defenses against increasingly sophisticated threats, and create recovery systems that enable you to reclaim control even after security incidents occur.

Understanding the Digital Financial Landscape

The evolution of money from physical currency to digital assets has created unprecedented opportunities for wealth building while simultaneously introducing complex security challenges that previous generations never faced. Your financial life now exists across multiple digital platforms, each representing both gateway to prosperity and potential vulnerability to exploitation.

This digital transformation affects every aspect of financial management, from basic banking and investment activities to emerging opportunities in cryptocurrency, digital payments, and online business operations. Understanding this landscape enables strategic thinking about security measures that protect your wealth without limiting your ability to capitalize on digital financial opportunities.

The interconnected nature of modern financial systems means that a security breach in one area can cascade across your entire financial life, making comprehensive security strategies essential rather than optional for anyone serious about building and protecting wealth in the digital age.

The New Threat Environment

Digital financial threats have evolved far beyond simple password theft to encompass sophisticated social engineering, advanced persistent threats, and systemic attacks that target entire financial infrastructures rather than individual accounts, requiring more comprehensive security approaches.

Cybercriminals now operate with business-like efficiency, targeting high-value individuals and developing specialized attacks that exploit human psychology as much as technical vulnerabilities, making awareness and education critical components of effective security strategies.

The global nature of digital threats means that attacks can originate anywhere in the world while targeting your local financial accounts, requiring security measures that account for international cybercrime organizations and state-sponsored hacking activities that traditional security advice may not address.

Understanding Attack Vectors

Phishing attacks have become increasingly sophisticated, using artificial intelligence to create convincing impersonations of legitimate institutions while exploiting emotional triggers like urgency, fear, or greed to bypass rational security thinking and trick victims into revealing sensitive information.

Malware and ransomware specifically target financial information and cryptocurrency wallets, with some variants designed to remain dormant until they detect significant financial activity, making continuous protection and monitoring essential for anyone with substantial digital assets.

Social engineering attacks exploit human relationships and trust to gain access to financial accounts, often targeting family members, friends, or professional associates to obtain information that enables account compromise through seemingly legitimate channels.

Digital Asset Evolution

Cryptocurrency and digital assets represent both significant opportunities and unique security challenges, requiring specialized knowledge about wallet security, private key management, and blockchain-specific threats that traditional financial security measures do not address.

The irreversible nature of many digital transactions means that security mistakes often cannot be corrected through traditional channels like bank disputes or insurance claims, making prevention far more critical than recovery in the digital asset space.

Emerging financial technologies including decentralized finance (DeFi), non-fungible tokens (NFTs), and digital identity systems create new categories of valuable digital assets that require evolving security strategies to protect against threats that are still being discovered and understood.

Regulatory and Insurance Gaps

Traditional consumer protections may not apply to digital assets and cryptocurrency holdings, leaving investors responsible for their own security without recourse through banks, government agencies, or insurance companies that provide protections for traditional financial assets.

The regulatory uncertainty surrounding digital assets creates additional risks as changing laws and enforcement priorities can affect asset accessibility, platform availability, and legal protections that investors might reasonably expect based on traditional financial experience.

International jurisdiction issues complicate recovery efforts when security breaches involve assets held on foreign platforms or stolen by criminals operating across national boundaries, making prevention and self-reliance essential for digital asset security.

Protecting Your Digital Wallets and Accounts

Securing your digital financial assets requires layered approaches that combine technical security measures with behavioral practices and strategic planning that create multiple barriers to unauthorized access while maintaining convenient access for legitimate financial activities.

This protection must extend across all your digital financial touchpoints, from traditional banking apps and investment platforms to cryptocurrency wallets and emerging financial technologies, ensuring comprehensive coverage that adapts to evolving threats and expanding digital asset portfolios.

Understanding wallet security principles enables you to make informed decisions about platform selection, security tool implementation, and risk management strategies that protect your wealth while enabling participation in digital financial opportunities that support your wealth-building objectives.

Banking and Investment Account Security

Multifactor authentication represents the minimum security standard for any account containing significant financial assets, providing additional verification layers that prevent unauthorized access even when passwords are compromised through data breaches or phishing attacks.

Strong password practices include unique passwords for each financial account, preferably generated and stored using reputable password managers that create complex credentials impossible to guess or remember, eliminating password reuse that creates vulnerabilities across multiple accounts.

Account monitoring through regular review of statements, transaction alerts, and credit reports enables early detection of unauthorized activity while providing evidence for dispute resolution and fraud reporting that may be time-sensitive for successful resolution.

Advanced Account Protection

Dedicated devices for financial activities create isolated environments that reduce exposure to malware and other threats that might compromise credentials or transaction data, particularly valuable for high-net-worth individuals managing significant digital assets.

VPN usage for financial transactions adds encryption layers that protect data transmission from interception, particularly important when accessing financial accounts from public networks or while traveling internationally where network security may be compromised.

Geographic restrictions and travel notifications inform financial institutions about expected activity patterns while enabling them to identify and block suspicious transactions that occur outside normal usage patterns or geographic locations.

Cryptocurrency Wallet Security

Cold storage solutions keep cryptocurrency private keys offline and disconnected from internet-accessible devices, providing maximum security for long-term holdings while requiring careful procedures for accessing funds that balance security with usability.

Hardware wallets offer secure storage solutions that keep private keys on dedicated devices designed specifically for cryptocurrency security, providing convenient access while maintaining security standards that software wallets cannot match due to their exposure to internet-connected environments.

Multi-signature requirements for significant transactions add additional approval layers that prevent unauthorized transfers while providing protection against both external threats and internal mistakes that might result in irreversible asset losses.

Private Key Management

Seed phrase security requires physical storage of recovery words in secure locations separate from devices and internet-connected systems, often involving multiple copies stored in different locations to prevent total loss from fire, theft, or natural disasters.

Key rotation strategies involve periodically moving assets to new wallets with fresh private keys, reducing exposure time for any single key while providing opportunities to verify backup procedures and maintain security hygiene over extended periods.

Inheritance planning for cryptocurrency requires secure transfer of private key information to trusted parties without compromising current security, often involving legal structures or technical solutions that enable asset recovery by heirs without creating vulnerabilities during the owner's lifetime.

Mobile and Digital Payment Security

Device security settings including screen locks, automatic updates, and app permissions create foundational protections for mobile devices that handle financial transactions, preventing unauthorized access and ensuring security patches are applied promptly.

App selection criteria should prioritize official applications from recognized financial institutions and cryptocurrency projects while avoiding third-party apps that may contain malware or security vulnerabilities that compromise financial information or transaction security.

Transaction verification procedures involve reviewing all payment details before confirming transfers, particularly important for cryptocurrency transactions that cannot be reversed once confirmed on blockchain networks, requiring careful attention to recipient addresses and amounts.

Secure Payment Practices

Public Wi-Fi avoidance for financial transactions prevents network-based attacks that can intercept financial data or inject malicious code into financial applications, requiring either cellular data or trusted private networks for any financial activity.

Regular app updates ensure that security patches are applied promptly while removing outdated applications that may contain known vulnerabilities, maintaining current security standards across all financial applications and reducing attack surface area.

Backup and recovery procedures ensure that financial access can be restored if devices are lost, stolen, or damaged, requiring secure storage of recovery information that enables account access without compromising security through easily discoverable backup data.

Phishing Defense and Social Engineering Protection

Modern phishing attacks exploit sophisticated psychological manipulation combined with technical precision to create convincing impersonations of legitimate financial institutions, making recognition and resistance skills essential for maintaining financial security in the digital age.

These attacks often combine multiple channels including email, text messages, phone calls, and social media to create persistent pressure while using urgency, fear, authority, or greed to override rational security thinking and trick victims into revealing sensitive financial information.

Developing resistance to social engineering requires understanding both the technical aspects of how these attacks work and the psychological principles they exploit, enabling you to maintain security awareness even under emotional pressure or convincing impersonation attempts.

Recognizing Phishing Attempts

Email phishing indicators include suspicious sender addresses, urgent language demanding immediate action, requests for sensitive information that legitimate institutions would never request via email, and links to websites that impersonate but don't exactly match official financial institution domains.

Text message and phone scams often claim to represent your bank, credit card company, or government agency while requesting account verification information or immediate action to prevent account closure, using fear and urgency to pressure quick responses without careful verification.

Website spoofing creates convincing replicas of legitimate financial login pages designed to capture credentials when victims attempt to log in, requiring careful URL verification and bookmark usage to ensure connection to authentic financial institution websites.

Advanced Detection Techniques

Header analysis in suspicious emails can reveal true sender information and routing details that expose fraudulent messages attempting to impersonate legitimate financial institutions, though this requires some technical knowledge to interpret effectively.

Link analysis involves checking destination URLs before clicking while hovering over links to preview actual destinations, ensuring that links lead to legitimate websites rather than spoofed pages designed to steal credentials or install malware.

Grammar and formatting analysis often reveals inconsistencies in professional communications that indicate fraudulent messages, as legitimate financial institutions maintain high standards for customer communications that scammers often fail to replicate convincingly.

Social Engineering Defense

Verification procedures require independent confirmation of any suspicious contact claiming to represent financial institutions, involving calling official customer service numbers from legitimate sources rather than responding to potentially fraudulent contact attempts.

Information limitation involves never providing sensitive financial information in response to unsolicited contact, regardless of how convincing the request appears, maintaining strict policies about information sharing that prevent successful social engineering attempts.

Authority resistance involves maintaining healthy skepticism even when contacted by individuals claiming official authority or urgent situations, recognizing that legitimate institutions provide time for careful consideration rather than demanding immediate responses to threats.

Psychological Manipulation Recognition

Urgency tactics create artificial time pressure designed to prevent careful consideration of suspicious requests, requiring conscious recognition that legitimate financial matters rarely require immediate action without time for proper verification and consideration.

Authority exploitation involves criminals impersonating government officials, bank executives, or law enforcement to intimidate victims into compliance, requiring understanding that legitimate authorities follow proper procedures rather than demanding immediate phone or email responses.

Fear manipulation includes threats of account closure, legal action, or financial penalties designed to override rational thinking, requiring recognition that legitimate institutions communicate threats through official channels rather than unsolicited contact attempts.

Building Security Awareness

Regular security training through reputable cybersecurity resources keeps you informed about evolving threats while building recognition skills that enable identification of new attack methods before they become widespread or personally threatening.

Simulation exercises involving intentional exposure to example phishing attempts help build recognition skills in safe environments while testing your ability to identify threats without risk of actual compromise or financial loss.

Community awareness involves sharing threat information with friends, family, and professional networks while learning from others' experiences with security incidents that might reveal new attack methods or protective strategies worth implementing.

Organizational Security Culture

Family security education ensures that all household members understand security principles and practices that protect shared financial resources while preventing successful attacks that target less security-conscious family members to gain access to shared accounts or information.

Professional network security involves maintaining security awareness in business relationships while avoiding discussions of financial details or security practices that might be exploited by criminals conducting research for targeted attacks.

Reporting suspicious activity to appropriate authorities helps combat cybercrime while potentially preventing other victims from falling victim to the same attacks, contributing to broader cybersecurity awareness and law enforcement efforts.

Cold Storage and Secure Offline Practices

Cold storage represents the ultimate security measure for digital assets, keeping private keys and sensitive financial information completely disconnected from internet-accessible devices while maintaining the ability to access funds when necessary through carefully controlled procedures.

This approach provides maximum security for long-term cryptocurrency holdings and backup financial information while requiring systematic procedures for accessing stored assets that balance security requirements with practical usability for legitimate financial activities.

Understanding cold storage principles enables strategic decisions about which assets require offline protection while developing procedures that maintain security without creating impractical barriers to necessary financial activities or emergency access requirements.

Physical Security Measures

Hardware wallet storage requires secure physical locations that protect devices from theft, fire, water damage, and other environmental threats while maintaining accessibility for legitimate use without creating security vulnerabilities through predictable storage patterns.

Safe deposit boxes provide professional security for backup information and recovery materials while requiring careful consideration of access procedures, bank policies, and disaster recovery scenarios that might affect availability during emergencies.

Geographic distribution of backup materials prevents total loss from localized disasters while requiring coordination between multiple storage locations that maintain security while enabling recovery from any single storage location failure or inaccessibility.

Environmental Protection

Fire and water resistance for stored materials requires protective containers or storage methods that maintain information integrity through common disaster scenarios while preventing degradation over extended storage periods that might alter readability or usability.

Temperature and humidity control prevents degradation of storage media while ensuring long-term reliability of backup information stored in various formats, from paper documents to electronic storage devices that may be sensitive to environmental conditions.

Tamper evidence systems enable detection of unauthorized access attempts to stored materials while providing confidence that backup information has not been compromised during storage periods between access events for legitimate purposes.

Backup and Recovery Systems

Multi-location backup strategies distribute recovery information across multiple secure locations while ensuring that no single point of failure can prevent asset recovery, requiring coordination between storage locations while maintaining security at each site.

Recovery testing procedures verify that backup information remains accessible and accurate while identifying potential problems before emergency situations when reliable recovery becomes critical for financial security or asset access.

Time-locked access systems provide additional security layers for backup materials while preventing impulsive access that might compromise security, requiring predetermined waiting periods that enable careful consideration of security implications before accessing stored information.

Professional Storage Solutions

Third-party custody services provide professional security for high-value digital assets while maintaining control over access decisions, requiring careful selection of reputable providers with appropriate insurance, security standards, and regulatory compliance.

Safe deposit box alternatives include private vault services and secure storage facilities that offer specialized services for digital asset backup materials while providing enhanced security features that traditional bank safe deposit boxes may not offer.

Legal structures for backup access enable trusted parties to access stored information under specific circumstances without compromising current security, requiring legal planning that addresses various scenarios while maintaining appropriate protective measures.

Air-Gapped Systems

Dedicated offline devices for sensitive financial operations create completely isolated environments that never connect to the internet while maintaining capability for necessary financial activities through controlled data transfer procedures that prevent network-based attacks.

Offline transaction signing enables secure authorization of financial transactions without exposing private keys to internet-connected devices while requiring systematic procedures for transaction preparation, signing, and broadcast that maintain security throughout the process.

Isolated backup creation ensures that sensitive financial information is processed and stored without network exposure while maintaining current backup information through periodic updates that follow secure procedures for data transfer and verification.

Operational Security Procedures

Clean room environments for sensitive operations prevent contamination from potentially compromised devices or networks while providing controlled spaces for handling sensitive financial information without risk of exposure or compromise.

Procedure documentation ensures consistent security practices while enabling others to follow necessary procedures in emergency situations that require asset recovery or financial access by trusted parties following predetermined protocols.

Regular security audits of offline storage and procedures identify potential vulnerabilities while ensuring that security measures remain effective against evolving threats that might require updates to storage methods or access procedures.

Online Financial Behavior Best Practices

Safe online financial behavior requires systematic approaches to every digital interaction that might affect your financial security, from routine banking activities to research about investment opportunities that may expose you to targeted attacks or fraudulent schemes.

These practices must become habitual behaviors that protect your financial interests without creating excessive inconvenience or limiting your ability to participate effectively in digital financial opportunities that support your wealth-building objectives and financial management needs.

Understanding behavioral security enables you to make informed decisions about online activities while developing habits that provide comprehensive protection without requiring constant conscious security decisions that might lead to security fatigue or inconsistent practices.

Safe Browsing Practices

Bookmark usage for financial websites eliminates the risk of typing errors or search result manipulation that might direct you to fraudulent sites designed to steal credentials while providing quick access to legitimate financial institution websites through verified links.

URL verification before entering sensitive information involves checking website addresses for exact matches to known legitimate sites while looking for subtle variations or suspicious elements that might indicate fraudulent websites attempting to steal financial information.

HTTPS verification ensures encrypted connections for all financial activities while providing confidence that data transmission is protected from interception, requiring attention to browser security indicators and warnings about potentially unsafe connections.

Browser Security Configuration

Ad blockers prevent exposure to malicious advertisements that might contain malware or direct to fraudulent financial websites while reducing distractions that might interfere with careful attention to security details during financial activities.

Script blocking tools provide control over website functionality while preventing potentially malicious code from executing, requiring some technical understanding to balance security with website functionality for legitimate financial services.

Privacy settings configuration limits data collection and tracking that might be used to build profiles for targeted attacks while maintaining functionality needed for legitimate financial services and applications.

Email and Communication Security

Email security practices include verification of sender authenticity before responding to any message requesting financial information or action while maintaining awareness that email addresses can be spoofed to appear legitimate when they are not.

Attachment handling requires extreme caution with any file received via email, particularly from unknown senders or unexpected messages from known contacts who might have compromised accounts, requiring virus scanning and sandboxed opening procedures for suspicious files.

Protect yourself by verifying email links. Before clicking, carefully examine the link's destination, and access the mentioned website directly through your browser rather than clicking the link.

Chapter 14: Emotional Recovery After Financial Collapse—The Phoenix Ledger

> *"In the sacred alchemy of collapse and rebirth, your financial ruin becomes the fertile soil from which your greatest wisdom grows. You are not broken—you are breaking open, transforming through the crucible of experience into someone who understands both the fragility and the resilience of the human spirit."*

In this chapter we walk you through a sanctuary of healing where your financial wounds are honored, your pain acknowledged, and your capacity for transformation celebrated. Here, within these compassionate pages, we embark upon a journey that recognizes financial collapse not as personal failure but as profound initiation—a doorway through which you must pass to discover the unshakable strength that lies dormant within your spirit.

As we venture together into this healing exploration, I invite you to release any self-judgment that whispers of inadequacy or shame. Instead, embrace the profound truth that emerges from these teachings: your financial collapse, however devastating it may feel, represents not your ending but your beginning—the first chapter of a comeback story that will inspire others and demonstrate the remarkable resilience of the human heart.

This chapter serves as your comprehensive guide through the emotional landscape of financial recovery, providing both practical tools and spiritual practices that honor the complexity of your healing journey. Together, we will explore how to transform shame into strength, rebuild trust in yourself and others, and create financial systems that feel supportive rather than punitive as you rise from the ashes of your former financial life.

Shame Detox: Releasing the Weight of Collapse

The weight of financial collapse extends far beyond numbers on bank statements or credit reports—it penetrates the very core of identity, creating wounds that require gentle attention and intentional healing before any practical rebuilding can begin with authentic strength and clarity.

Understanding shame as the silent destroyer of recovery enables its recognition and release, transforming the internal narrative from one of failure and unworthiness to one of resilience and wisdom earned through the most challenging of human experiences.

This detox process acknowledges that financial collapse often carries societal stigma that compounds personal pain, making it essential to separate your inherent worth from temporary circumstances while building the emotional foundation necessary for sustainable recovery.

Naming the Wound: Truth as Liberation

Financial collapse represents a rupture in the fabric of your expected life—a tearing away of security that reveals both vulnerability and previously unknown strength while demanding honest acknowledgment of what has been lost and what remains.

This naming process requires courage to face reality without the protective barriers of denial or minimization that might temporarily ease pain but ultimately delay healing and prevent the clear-eyed assessment necessary for strategic rebuilding.

The act of naming transforms abstract fear into concrete challenges while creating the possibility of resolution through direct engagement with truth that honors both the magnitude of loss and the potential for recovery.

Sacred Acknowledgment Practice

Journal exploration through structured prompts creates safe space for emotional processing while building comprehensive understanding of the collapse experience that includes both losses and hidden gifts discovered through adversity.

"What did I lose?" invites honest inventory of tangible and intangible losses including financial assets, relationships, dreams, and sense of security while acknowledging the full scope of impact without judgment or immediate problem-solving.

"What did I learn?" transforms pain into wisdom while identifying insights about money, relationships, personal strength, and life priorities that might never have emerged without the catalyst of financial crisis.

"What do I reclaim?" focuses energy on recovery while identifying values, goals, and aspects of identity that remain intact despite financial circumstances, creating foundation for rebuilding that honors authentic self rather than external expectations.

Detoxing Shame: Breaking the Silence of Suffering

Shame thrives in isolation and silence, growing stronger through secrecy while diminishing rapidly when exposed to compassionate witness and truthful sharing that reveals the universal nature of financial struggle and human vulnerability.

This detox requires distinguishing between guilt about specific actions and shame about fundamental worth, addressing actionable regrets while releasing the toxic belief that financial circumstances define personal value or future potential.

Community connection becomes essential medicine, providing perspective that normalizes struggle while offering support that validates experience and provides hope through shared stories of recovery and resilience.

Shame Release Rituals

Letter writing to your former self creates opportunity for compassion while expressing understanding for the person who made decisions based on available information and circumstances that seemed reasonable at the time they were made.

Fire ceremony that burns these letters transforms symbolic release into physical action while creating sacred space for letting go of self-judgment that no longer serves recovery or forward movement toward financial healing.

Story sharing within trusted community breaks shame's power while building connection and mutual support that transforms individual struggle into collective strength and shared wisdom about navigating financial challenges.

Reclaiming Identity: Beyond the Numbers

Your worth exists independently of credit scores, bank balances, or debt amounts while encompassing qualities of character, relationships, skills, and potential that remain intact regardless of financial circumstances or external judgments.

Identity reconstruction requires conscious choice about which aspects of personality and values will define your recovery while releasing outdated beliefs about success that might have contributed to unsustainable financial practices or unrealistic expectations.

This reclamation process builds foundation for financial decisions aligned with authentic values rather than external pressure, creating sustainable wealth-building approaches that honor individual strengths and limitations while supporting long-term well-being.

Identity Rebuilding Framework

Value clarification through reflective exercises identifies core beliefs about money, success, and fulfillment while distinguishing between personally meaningful goals and societal expectations that might not align with authentic desires or sustainable lifestyle.

Strength inventory documents skills, qualities, and resources that survived financial collapse while building confidence in capability to rebuild through strategic application of existing assets and continued development of valuable abilities.

Vision creation for future identity encompasses both financial goals and personal growth while painting comprehensive picture of recovery that includes material security and emotional well-being through balanced approach to reconstruction.

Comeback Rituals: Rebuilding with Rhythm and Intention

Recovery from financial collapse requires more than practical strategy—it demands ritualistic practices that honor the healing process while creating emotional safety and spiritual strength that supports sustained effort through challenging periods of rebuilding.

These sacred practices acknowledge that financial recovery involves both external actions and internal transformation, requiring attention to emotional well-being alongside practical financial planning that addresses root causes rather than symptoms alone.

Ritualized approach to recovery creates structure and meaning that transforms overwhelming reconstruction into manageable daily practices while building momentum through consistent action that honors both progress and process.

Daily Grounding Rituals: Emotional Foundation

Morning practices that center your nervous system before engaging with financial reality create optimal conditions for clear thinking while preventing anxiety from overwhelming rational assessment of circumstances and available options.

These grounding rituals acknowledge that financial information can trigger intense emotional responses that interfere with strategic thinking, making emotional preparation essential for productive engagement with recovery tasks and decision-making.

Consistent daily practice builds emotional resilience while creating positive associations with financial attention that replace avoidance patterns with curious engagement that supports rather than undermines recovery progress.

Morning Centering Practices

Breathwork before checking balances calms nervous system while creating intentional space between emotional reaction and financial information, enabling clearer assessment and more strategic response to daily financial realities.

Gratitude journaling for non-monetary wealth builds awareness of resources beyond money while maintaining perspective that prevents financial circumstances from overshadowing other forms of abundance and support available in life.

Money altar creation with symbols of abundance, resilience, and rebirth provides visual reminder of recovery intention while creating sacred space that honors both struggle and strength within the rebuilding process.

Financial Re-Entry Plan: Strategic Recovery

Systematic approach to financial reconstruction prevents overwhelm while creating manageable steps that build confidence through small victories that demonstrate progress and capability during vulnerable recovery period.

This planning process emphasizes micro-wins that provide immediate positive reinforcement while building toward larger goals through accumulated success that proves ability to manage money responsibly and strategically despite past challenges.

Progress tracking through visual systems provides motivation while creating accountability that maintains momentum during difficult periods when progress might feel slow or insufficient compared to the magnitude of loss experienced.

Structured Recovery Implementation

Step One involves inventory without judgment that documents current financial reality including assets, debts, and obligations while gathering information necessary for strategic planning without emotional overwhelm or self-criticism.

Step Two focuses on micro-wins including small savings amounts, single debt communications, or budget line clarifications that provide immediate success while building financial management skills through low-risk practice and positive reinforcement.

Step Three creates comeback calendar that tracks rituals, milestones, and emotional check-ins while providing structure that supports consistent progress through visual representation of effort and achievement over time.

Community Support: Shared Strength

Recovery thrives within supportive community that understands the unique challenges of financial collapse while providing both emotional support and practical guidance from others who have navigated similar experiences successfully.

This community connection breaks isolation while providing accountability and encouragement that sustains effort through difficult periods when individual motivation might waver or external circumstances create additional stress.

Professional support through financial trauma-informed coaches provides specialized expertise while peer support through group experiences creates belonging and shared wisdom that accelerates healing through collective strength and mutual aid.

Community Building Strategy

Support group identification through financial recovery organizations provides structured environments while connecting with others who understand the emotional complexity of financial collapse and reconstruction challenges.

Accountability partnership with trusted individuals creates mutual support while sharing progress and challenges that maintain momentum through difficult periods and celebrate victories that might otherwise go unrecognized.

Story sharing that transforms personal pain into community blueprint provides meaning while helping others navigate similar challenges through lived experience and practical wisdom earned through recovery process.

Rebuilding Trust: With Self, Systems, and Others

Trust destruction represents one of the most profound impacts of financial collapse, affecting confidence in personal judgment, faith in financial systems, and belief in others' support during vulnerable periods of reconstruction and healing.

Rebuilding trust requires patient attention to both rational assessment and emotional healing while developing discernment that protects against future harm without creating isolation that prevents beneficial relationships and opportunities.

This reconstruction process acknowledges that trust must be earned through consistent experience while creating frameworks for evaluation that support wise decision-making throughout recovery and beyond.

Trusting Yourself Again: Internal Compass Restoration

Self-trust reconstruction begins with honest assessment of decision-making patterns while identifying both mistakes and sound judgment that led to financial collapse, creating balanced perspective that acknowledges responsibility without overwhelming self-condemnation.

This process requires relearning to distinguish between intuitive wisdom and emotional reactivity while developing confidence in ability to make sound financial decisions based on current circumstances rather than past mistakes or future fears.

Emotional intelligence development through mood tracking and pattern recognition builds awareness of internal states that affect financial decision-making while creating strategies for optimal timing and approach to important financial choices.

Self-Trust Development Practices

Money mood logging tracks emotional states before and after financial activities while building awareness of triggers and patterns that might compromise judgment or create unnecessary stress during recovery period.

Decision celebration acknowledges every choice made with clarity while building confidence through recognition of sound judgment even in small matters that demonstrate growing competence and trustworthiness.

Instinct training through small financial decisions builds confidence while providing low-risk opportunities to practice judgment and evaluate outcomes that strengthen trust in personal capability and wisdom.

Trusting Systems with Strategic Caution

System re-engagement requires education about rules and requirements while building understanding that enables strategic navigation without naive trust that might lead to future vulnerability or exploitation.

This approach balances healthy skepticism with practical engagement while using protective measures that maintain agency and control throughout interactions with financial institutions and legal systems.

Automation serves strategic purposes while maintaining sovereignty through regular review and adjustment that ensures systems serve individual interests rather than creating passive dependency that might compromise future flexibility.

System Engagement Framework

Rule learning about credit, banking, and taxes provides knowledge necessary for strategic interaction while understanding requirements and opportunities that enable optimal outcomes within existing frameworks.

Automation implementation reduces overwhelming decision-making while maintaining control through regular review that ensures automated systems continue serving recovery goals rather than operating independently of conscious intention.

Protective boundaries that limit exposure while enabling necessary engagement create safety while building experience that demonstrates system navigation capability without excessive risk or vulnerability.

Trusting Others: Relationship Reconstruction

Relationship trust requires careful evaluation of trustworthiness while rebuilding capacity for appropriate vulnerability that enables mutual support without exposing recovery process to those who might not understand or support financial healing.

This reconstruction process involves teaching others about recovery needs while establishing boundaries that protect emotional and financial well-being during vulnerable periods when additional stress could compromise progress.

Financial intimacy restoration occurs gradually through transparent communication while building shared understanding that honors both individual recovery needs and relationship requirements for mutual trust and support.

Relationship Trust Building

Boundary establishment around shared money and financial expectations creates safety while protecting recovery process from external pressure that might compromise individual healing or create conflict within supportive relationships.

Transparency practices that share appropriate information build understanding while maintaining privacy around details that might not be necessary for relationship support but could create unnecessary concern or judgment.

Teaching opportunities that share recovery lessons transform personal experience into relationship strengthening while building mutual understanding that benefits both individual healing and collective financial wisdom.

Case Studies of Resilience & Rebirth

These stories illuminate the transformative potential within financial collapse while demonstrating that recovery not only restores previous financial position but often creates opportunities for greater success than existed before the crisis occurred.

Each narrative reveals unique pathways through recovery while highlighting common themes of resilience, creativity, and community that enable transformation of devastating loss into powerful comeback stories that inspire others.

Understanding these journeys provides hope while demonstrating practical strategies that others have used successfully to rebuild financial security and create meaningful work that serves both personal recovery and community contribution.

The Artist's Phoenix: From Divorce Loss to Creative Empire

Sarah's story begins with devastating divorce that resulted in loss of home, savings, and shared business while leaving her with minimal resources and overwhelming grief that initially paralyzed creative output and financial planning capability.

The transformation occurred through channeling emotional pain into artistic expression while developing business skills that enabled monetization of creative work through strategic marketing and authentic storytelling that resonated with audiences.

Her six-figure brand emerged from willingness to share vulnerability while building community around shared experience of loss and recovery that created market demand for both artistic products and inspirational content about resilience.

Key Recovery Elements

Emotional processing through art created therapeutic outlet while generating products that became foundation for business development that honored both personal healing and market demand for authentic creative expression.

Business education through online courses and mentorship provided practical skills while building confidence in capability to manage financial aspects of creative work without sacrificing artistic integrity or authenticity.

Community building through social media sharing created audience while establishing thought leadership in creative recovery that generated income through multiple streams including art sales, coaching, and speaking opportunities.

The Freelancer's Transformation: From Bankruptcy to Teaching

Michael's bankruptcy resulted from medical crisis that combined health challenges with business collapse while creating overwhelming debt that seemed insurmountable despite years of successful freelance work and responsible financial management.

Recovery began with systematic debt resolution while rebuilding freelance income through strategic skill development that enabled higher rates and more selective client relationships based on value creation rather than desperation for income.

His teaching career emerged from recognition that his recovery experience provided valuable insights for other freelancers while creating scalable income through course development and coaching that served underserved neurodivergent creative community.

Transformation Strategies

Skill specialization in high-demand areas enabled premium pricing while building reputation for expertise that attracted ideal clients willing to pay appropriately for valuable services and strategic guidance.

System development for freelance financial management created frameworks that prevented future crises while providing teachable content that became foundation for educational products and services.

Community service through financial education created fulfillment while building business opportunities that served both recovery goals and meaningful contribution to others facing similar challenges.

The Parent's Cooperative: From Credit Rebuild to Community Leadership

Maria's journey began with single parenthood and credit destruction that limited housing options while creating daily stress about providing stability for children during economically challenging transition period.

Systematic credit repair through education and strategic planning enabled improved financial position while building confidence in ability to navigate complex financial systems and advocate effectively for family needs.

Her community cooperative emerged from recognition that shared resources could benefit multiple families while creating business opportunities that served both individual financial recovery and collective community strengthening through mutual aid.

Community Impact Elements

Credit education sharing helped other parents while building expertise that became foundation for consulting services that provided income while serving community need for financial literacy and empowerment.

Cooperative development created resource sharing while enabling business ownership that generated income through group purchasing power and collective services that benefited all members.

Mentorship programs that support others through financial recovery created legacy while building network of mutual support that strengthens entire community through shared wisdom and collaborative problem-solving.

Phoenix Creed for Financial Rebirth

This creed serves as your declaration of transformation while establishing principles that guide recovery decisions and identity reconstruction through empowering language that honors both struggle and strength within the rebuilding process.

These affirmations acknowledge the reality of collapse while claiming agency in recovery process that transforms victim identity into hero's journey of personal growth and financial wisdom earned through direct experience of challenge and triumph.

Integration of these concepts into daily practice provides emotional anchor while building confidence that supports sustained effort through challenging periods when doubt or discouragement might threaten commitment to recovery goals.

Sacred Affirmations of Rising

Your burning represents purification rather than destruction while acknowledging that collapse cleared away unsustainable patterns and beliefs that might have prevented authentic success and fulfillment in previous financial approaches.

Breaking describes the opening of possibility rather than damage while recognizing that rigid structures and expectations had to dissolve before flexible and responsive approaches to wealth-building could emerge from recovery experience.

Shame burial creates space for wisdom while transforming self-condemnation into self-compassion that enables clear thinking and strategic action based on current reality rather than past mistakes or future fears.

Identity Transformation Declaration

Rising "as I choose to be" claims agency while refusing to accept limitation based on past circumstances or external expectations that might not align with authentic values and recovery goals.

Chapter 15: The Future of Investing

"The future is not a destination to be reached, but a reality to be co-created. The seeds of tomorrow's prosperity are sown in the fertile ground of today's imagination, innovation, and courage."

Let us peer together beyond the present, into the horizon where possibility unfolds. In this chapter, we embark on a journey into the future of investing—a landscape being reshaped by breathtaking technological advancements and a profound shift in human values. My hope is to offer you not a crystal ball, but a compass; a tool to help you navigate the emerging trends with wisdom, curiosity, and a sense of profound opportunity.

As we explore this new world together, I invite you to hold two ideas in harmony. First, the timeless principles of discipline, patience, and diversification remain your steadfast anchors. Second, the currents of innovation are not to be feared, but to be understood and harnessed. The future of investing belongs to those who can build upon a strong foundation while courageously embracing the transformative power of change. May these pages illuminate your path and inspire you to become a conscious architect of your own financial destiny.

The Rise of Decentralized Finance (DeFi)

Imagine a financial system that is open to everyone, without intermediaries, gatekeepers, or centralized control. This is the revolutionary promise of Decentralized Finance, or DeFi. Built upon the foundation of blockchain technology, DeFi aims to recreate traditional financial services—like lending, borrowing, and exchanging assets—in a permissionless and transparent way.

At its core, DeFi replaces banks and brokerage firms with smart contracts, which are self-executing programs that run on a blockchain. This creates a system that is not only more efficient but also more accessible. For centuries, the global financial system has been defined by walls and barriers. DeFi is a powerful movement working to dismantle those walls, offering opportunities for individuals who have historically been excluded.

- **Opportunities:** DeFi opens up new avenues for earning returns, such as providing liquidity to decentralized exchanges or lending your assets directly to others in return for interest. It offers a level of transparency that is unheard of in traditional finance, as all transactions are recorded on a public ledger.

- **Risks:** This frontier is not without its perils. The technology is still nascent and can be complex. Smart contracts can have vulnerabilities that bad actors can exploit, and regulatory uncertainty remains a significant concern. The high volatility of the crypto assets that power DeFi also presents a substantial risk.

To engage with DeFi is to step into a world of incredible innovation. It requires a commitment to continuous learning and a healthy respect for the risks involved. Yet, its potential to democratize finance makes it one of the most exciting and important trends shaping our future.

Tokenization of Assets

Throughout history, investing in high-value assets like commercial real estate, fine art, or rare collectibles has been a privilege reserved for the ultra-wealthy. The barriers to entry—high capital requirements and lack of access—were simply too great. Tokenization is changing that narrative forever.

Tokenization is the process of creating a digital representation, or "token," of a real-world asset on a blockchain. This token can then be divided into smaller fractions, allowing multiple people to own a piece of the underlying asset. Think of it as creating a thousand digital shares of a single Picasso painting or a skyscraper in Manhattan.

This innovation is unlocking a universe of previously illiquid assets, making them accessible to everyday investors.

- **Real Estate:** Instead of needing millions to buy an apartment building, you can purchase tokens representing a small ownership stake, entitling you to a share of the rental income and property appreciation.

- **Fine Art and Collectibles:** Platforms are emerging that allow you to buy fractional shares of iconic artworks or rare memorabilia, giving you a chance to participate in markets that were once exclusive.

- **Private Equity:** Tokenization can even be applied to shares in private, pre-IPO companies, giving smaller investors access to early-stage growth opportunities.

By breaking down large assets into small, affordable, and easily tradable digital tokens, tokenization is democratizing access to wealth creation. It represents a fundamental shift from a world where you had to be rich to invest in the best assets, to a world where you can invest in the best assets to become rich.

Artificial Intelligence in Investing

Artificial Intelligence (AI) is moving beyond the realm of science fiction and becoming a powerful co-pilot for investors. AI algorithms can process and analyze vast amounts of data—from market trends and financial reports to news sentiment and social media chatter—at a speed and scale that is impossible for the human mind. This capability is revolutionizing every aspect of the investment process.

- **Portfolio Management:** AI-powered "robo-advisors" are already providing low-cost, automated portfolio management based on your goals and risk tolerance. In the future, AI will offer even more sophisticated and personalized strategies, dynamically adjusting your portfolio in response to real-time market changes.

- **Risk Assessment:** AI can identify subtle patterns and correlations in market data to better predict and manage risk. It can flag potential downturns or identify over-leveraged positions, providing an early warning system for your investments.

- **Personalized Financial Advice:** Imagine having a personal financial advisor available 24/7, one that understands your unique financial situation, goals, and even your emotional biases. AI will make hyper-personalized financial guidance accessible to everyone, not just the wealthy.

The rise of AI does not make human wisdom obsolete. Rather, it enhances it. The future of investing will likely be a beautiful synergy between human intuition and machine intelligence, allowing us to make more informed, data-driven, and rational decisions on our path to financial well-being.

Sustainable and Impact Investing

One of the most heartening trends shaping the future of investing is a collective awakening of consciousness. A growing wave of investors is no longer asking only, "What is the financial return on my investment?" They are also asking, "What is the human and environmental impact of my investment?"

This has given rise to sustainable and impact investing, which involves aligning your financial portfolio with your personal values. This is often guided by ESG criteria, which evaluate a company's performance on:

- **Environmental** factors, such as its carbon footprint, pollution, and use of renewable energy.

- **Social** factors, including its labor practices, commitment to diversity and inclusion, and impact on the local community.

- **Governance** factors, like its board structure, executive compensation, and transparency.

What began as a niche interest has now entered the mainstream. The myth that you must sacrifice returns to invest responsibly is being dismantled. A growing body of evidence suggests that companies with strong ESG practices are often more resilient, innovative, and better positioned for long-term success.

This trend is a powerful reminder that capital has a voice. Where you choose to invest your money is a vote for the kind of world you want to live in. By investing in companies that are solving the world's biggest challenges—from climate change to social inequality—you are participating in a profound form of rebellion: using your wealth not just to serve yourself, but to serve humanity.

Preparing for the Future

Navigating this evolving landscape can feel both exhilarating and overwhelming. The key is not to have all the answers, but to cultivate a mindset of curiosity, adaptability, and lifelong learning. Here are a few actionable steps to help you prepare for the future of investing.

1. **Cultivate a Learning Mindset:** The world is changing faster than ever. Dedicate time each week to reading about these emerging trends. Follow thoughtful leaders in DeFi, AI, and sustainable investing. Listen to podcasts. Your greatest asset will be your ability to learn and adapt.

1. **Start Small and Experiment:** You don't have to dive into the deep end. Open an account on a reputable crypto exchange and use dollar-cost averaging to invest a small, manageable amount. Explore a real estate crowdfunding platform with a minimal investment. The experience you gain from these small experiments will be invaluable.

1. **Strengthen Your Foundation:** New technologies do not negate timeless principles. Before you venture into more speculative areas, ensure you have a solid core portfolio of low-cost, diversified index funds. A strong foundation gives you the stability to explore the frontiers with confidence.

1. **Embrace a Long-Term Vision:** Whether you are investing in a traditional index fund or a new DeFi protocol, a long-term perspective is crucial. The most transformative innovations

often experience the greatest short-term volatility. Resist the urge to react to market noise and remain focused on your long-term vision.

The future of investing is a tapestry woven from threads of technology, consciousness, and human ingenuity. It is a future that promises to be more democratic, more personalized, and more aligned with our deepest values. By embracing it with an open mind and a steady hand, you are not just positioning yourself for financial success—you are participating in the creation of a more equitable and abundant world for all. Your journey as a forward-thinking investor begins today.

Chapter 16: Projecting Investment Value

"The future belongs to those who can see it clearly today. While others guess and hope, the strategic investor calculates possibilities, weighs probabilities, and transforms uncertainty into opportunity through the disciplined art of value projection."

Step away from reactive market participation and embrace your role as an architect of your financial future. This chapter isn't just about crunching numbers; it's an invitation to a sophisticated realm where mathematical precision meets strategic vision, empowering you to make investment decisions with remarkable clarity and power.

As we venture together into this illuminating exploration, I invite you to embrace this knowledge with the curiosity of a detective and the ambition of an entrepreneur. The ability to project investment value represents one of the most crucial skills separating successful wealth builders from the countless others who stumble through financial markets hoping for favorable outcomes without systematic frameworks for evaluating opportunities and predicting results.

This chapter serves as your comprehensive guide to mastering the art and science of investment projection, providing you with analytical tools that transform abstract possibilities into concrete expectations while enabling strategic decision-making that aligns your investment choices with your deepest aspirations and most important life goals. Together, we will explore sophisticated frameworks that professional investors use to evaluate opportunities, time their decisions, and build wealth systematically through informed strategic positioning.

The Foundation of Value Projection: Understanding What You're Really Calculating

Investment value projection represents far more than simple mathematical exercises—it embodies the strategic thinking processes that enable informed decision-making under uncertainty while providing frameworks for comparing different opportunities and timing investment decisions for optimal outcomes. This analytical discipline transforms investment selection from guesswork into systematic evaluation based on evidence and reasoning.

The power of value projection lies not in its ability to predict the future with certainty, but in its capacity to organize thinking, clarify assumptions, and enable rational comparison of different investment alternatives under various scenarios. This structured approach provides confidence in decision-making while revealing the key variables that most significantly influence investment success.

Understanding value projection requires grasping both its mathematical foundations and its practical limitations, recognizing that projections represent estimates based on current information and assumptions that may change as conditions evolve. This balanced perspective enables effective use of projection tools while maintaining appropriate humility about the inherent uncertainty in all investment endeavors.

The Time Value of Money: Your Investment Foundation

Every projection framework rests upon the fundamental principle that money available today is worth more than the same amount available in the future, due to both inflation effects and opportunity costs that erode future purchasing power while creating alternatives for current capital deployment.

Understanding time value enables meaningful comparison between investment opportunities with different cash flow patterns, holding periods, and risk characteristics by converting all future values to present-day equivalents that can be compared directly. This mathematical foundation provides the basis for sophisticated investment analysis.

The time value concept also underlies the critical relationship between risk and return, as investors demand higher returns for accepting greater uncertainty or longer time commitments that delay access to their capital while exposing it to various risks that could prevent expected outcomes from materializing.

Present Value and Future Value Calculations

Present value calculations determine what future cash flows are worth in today's dollars, enabling comparison of investments with different timing characteristics while accounting for the opportunity cost of capital deployment over specific periods. This calculation forms the foundation for most sophisticated valuation methods.

Future value calculations project what current investments might be worth at specific future dates, enabling goal-setting and planning while revealing the compound growth patterns that create long-term wealth accumulation through disciplined investing over extended periods.

The discount rate used in these calculations reflects the rate of return available from alternative investments with similar risk characteristics, providing the benchmark against which specific opportunities are evaluated. Selecting appropriate discount rates requires understanding both market conditions and personal risk tolerance.

Risk and Return Relationships in Projection

All investment projections must account for the fundamental relationship between risk and expected return, as higher returns typically require accepting greater uncertainty about actual outcomes while lower-risk investments generally offer more predictable but limited return potential.

This relationship affects projection methodology by requiring probability-weighted scenarios that consider multiple potential outcomes rather than single-point estimates that might create false precision about inherently uncertain future events. Scenario analysis provides more realistic frameworks for investment evaluation.

Understanding risk-return relationships also enables appropriate diversification strategies that balance portfolio-level risk and return characteristics while ensuring that individual investment projections consider their roles within broader strategic frameworks rather than as isolated decisions.

Systematic vs. Unsystematic Risk

Systematic risk affects all investments within markets or asset classes, creating correlated movements that cannot be eliminated through diversification while requiring compensation through higher expected returns for investors willing to accept market-wide uncertainty.

Unsystematic risk affects individual investments or sectors, creating uncertainty that can be reduced through diversification while potentially offering higher returns for investors willing to accept concentration risks through careful selection and active management.

Projection frameworks must consider both risk types when estimating expected returns and evaluating probability distributions around those estimates, as different risks require different analytical approaches and mitigation strategies that affect realistic return expectations.

Return on Investment (ROI): The Universal Performance Metric

Return on Investment represents the most fundamental metric for evaluating investment performance and projecting future outcomes, providing standardized frameworks for comparing different opportunities while measuring actual results against expectations and benchmarks.

ROI calculations transform absolute dollar gains or losses into percentage returns that enable meaningful comparison across investments of different sizes, types, and holding periods. This standardization provides essential tools for portfolio management and strategic decision-making while revealing which investments contribute most effectively to wealth-building objectives.

Understanding different ROI calculation methods and their appropriate applications enables more sophisticated analysis while avoiding common mistakes that can lead to incorrect conclusions about investment attractiveness or performance quality.

Basic ROI Calculations and Interpretations

The simplest ROI calculation divides investment gains by the initial investment amount, creating percentage returns that reveal how effectively capital has been deployed while providing comparative metrics for evaluating different investment opportunities.

Simple ROI Formula and Applications

Simple ROI equals (Final Value—Initial Investment) divided by Initial Investment, multiplied by 100 to express results as percentages. This calculation provides immediate insights into investment effectiveness while enabling comparison across different opportunities and time periods.

For example, an investment of $1,000 that grows to $1,200 generates an ROI of 20% ($200 gain divided by $1,000 initial investment). This percentage return enables direct comparison with other investments regardless of their absolute dollar amounts.

However, simple ROI calculations do not account for timing differences, making a 20% return achieved in one year more attractive than the same 20% return achieved over five years. This limitation requires more sophisticated calculations for accurate investment evaluation.

Annualized ROI and Time Adjustment

Annualized ROI calculations adjust returns for time differences, enabling meaningful comparison between investments with different holding periods while revealing the compound annual growth rates that drive long-term wealth accumulation.

The annualized ROI formula raises the total return ratio to the power of (1 divided by years held), then subtracts 1 to express the result as an annual percentage. This calculation reveals the compound annual growth rate that would produce the same total return over the investment period.

For example, a $1,000 investment that grows to $1,500 over three years generates a 50% total return, equivalent to an annualized ROI of approximately 14.5%. This annualized figure enables comparison with other investments regardless of their specific holding periods.

Advanced ROI Metrics and Applications

More sophisticated ROI metrics provide additional insights into investment quality and risk-adjusted performance while enabling more accurate projections and comparisons across different investment types and market conditions.

Risk-Adjusted Returns and Sharpe Ratios

Risk-adjusted return calculations account for the volatility and uncertainty associated with achieving specific returns, providing more complete assessments of investment attractiveness by considering both return potential and risk characteristics.

The Sharpe ratio divides excess returns (returns above risk-free rates) by the standard deviation of returns, creating metrics that reveal how much additional return is generated per unit of risk accepted. Higher Sharpe ratios indicate more efficient risk-return profiles.

These metrics enable comparison between investments with different risk characteristics while identifying opportunities that provide superior returns relative to their risk levels. Risk-adjusted analysis often reveals that lower-return, lower-risk investments provide better value than higher-return, higher-risk alternatives.

Internal Rate of Return (IRR) Analysis

Internal Rate of Return calculations determine the discount rate that makes the present value of investment cash flows equal to the initial investment amount, providing insights into the effective yield generated by specific investment opportunities.

IRR analysis proves particularly valuable for investments with irregular cash flow patterns, such as real estate investments that generate rental income plus eventual sale proceeds, or dividend-paying stocks that provide both income and capital appreciation over time.

Comparing IRRs across different investment opportunities enables selection of alternatives that generate the highest effective yields while considering factors such as liquidity, risk, and strategic fit within broader investment portfolios.

Time Horizon Analysis: Aligning Investments with Life Goals

Time horizon analysis represents one of the most crucial components of investment projection, as the length of time available for investments to compound significantly affects appropriate strategy selection, risk tolerance, and expected return parameters that guide decision-making.

Understanding how different time horizons affect investment dynamics enables strategic matching of investment approaches with specific financial goals while optimizing risk-return profiles for individual circumstances and objectives. This temporal perspective provides essential framework for all investment planning and projection activities.

Time horizon analysis also reveals the powerful effects of compound growth over extended periods, demonstrating how modest returns can create substantial wealth when given sufficient time to compound, while highlighting the challenges of achieving significant wealth accumulation over shorter periods.

Short-Term vs. Long-Term Projection Differences

Short-term investments face different constraints and opportunities compared to long-term investments, requiring modified projection approaches that account for reduced compounding periods, increased importance of timing, and different risk-return trade-offs that affect strategy selection.

Short-Term Investment Considerations (1-3 Years)

Short-term investments must prioritize capital preservation and liquidity while accepting limited return potential due to compressed time frames that prevent significant compound growth and require conservative positioning to ensure capital availability when needed.

Projection methods for short-term investments typically focus on realistic range estimates rather than aggressive growth scenarios, as the limited time available provides little opportunity to recover from adverse outcomes while requiring high probability of achieving projected returns.

Market timing becomes more important for short-term investments, as entry and exit timing significantly affects results when holdings periods are brief. This timing sensitivity requires different analytical approaches compared to long-term buy-and-hold strategies where timing effects tend to average out over time.

Long-Term Investment Advantages (5+ Years)

Long-term investments benefit from compound growth effects that can transform modest annual returns into substantial wealth accumulation over extended periods, while providing time to recover from temporary setbacks that might devastate short-term investment results.

The power of compounding becomes most apparent over longer time horizons, where even small differences in annual returns create dramatic differences in final outcomes. An investment growing at 8% annually versus 10% annually shows modest differences initially but substantial differences after decades of compounding.

Long-term projections can incorporate higher return assumptions and accept greater volatility because extended time periods provide opportunities to ride out market cycles while capturing the full benefit of equity risk premiums and economic growth that drive superior returns over time.

Goal-Based Time Horizon Planning

Matching investment time horizons with specific financial goals enables strategic portfolio construction that optimizes for different objectives while ensuring that investment approaches align with the timing and certainty requirements of various life goals and financial needs.

Education Funding Projections

Education funding represents a classic medium-term investment goal with relatively predictable timing and cost parameters that enable systematic planning and projection over 10-20 year periods, depending on children's ages and educational objectives.

Projection models for education funding must account for education cost inflation rates that typically exceed general inflation while incorporating assumptions about potential financial aid, scholarship opportunities, and family contribution expectations that affect net funding requirements.

Strategic asset allocation for education funding typically becomes more conservative as education dates approach, shifting from growth-oriented investments during early years to more stable, predictable investments as college enrollment nears and capital preservation becomes paramount.

Retirement Planning Projections

Retirement planning involves the longest time horizons for most investors, creating opportunities for aggressive growth strategies during early career phases while requiring gradual transition to income-focused approaches as retirement dates approach.

Retirement projections must account for inflation effects over multi-decade periods, longevity assumptions that affect withdrawal period planning, and lifestyle expectations that determine income replacement requirements for maintaining desired standards of living during retirement.

The extended time horizons available for retirement planning enable recovery from market downturns and economic cycles while providing opportunities to adjust strategies based on changing circumstances, career developments, and evolving financial priorities over working lifetimes.

Opportunity Cost: The Hidden Factor in Every Decision

Opportunity cost represents one of the most important yet frequently overlooked factors in investment analysis, as every investment decision inherently involves sacrificing alternative uses for the same capital that might generate different returns or provide different benefits.

Understanding opportunity cost enables more sophisticated investment evaluation by considering not just the absolute returns from specific investments, but the relative attractiveness compared to alternative opportunities available with similar risk characteristics and time commitments.

Opportunity cost analysis also provides frameworks for portfolio optimization and strategic decision-making by ensuring that capital allocation decisions consider the full range of available alternatives rather than focusing narrowly on individual investment evaluation in isolation.

Calculating and Applying Opportunity Cost

Opportunity cost calculations compare the returns from chosen investments against the returns available from the next-best alternatives, revealing whether investment decisions create value or destroy wealth relative to other available opportunities.

Comparative Return Analysis

The basic opportunity cost calculation subtracts the return from the next-best alternative from the return of the chosen investment, creating measures of value added or lost through specific investment decisions rather than accepting available alternatives.

For example, if a real estate investment generates 12% annual returns while available stock market investments generate 10% annual returns, the opportunity cost of choosing real estate is negative 2%, indicating value creation through superior investment selection.

However, opportunity cost calculations must account for risk differences between alternatives, as higher returns might simply reflect higher risks rather than superior investment skill or opportunity identification. Risk-adjusted opportunity cost provides more accurate evaluation frameworks.

Time and Liquidity Considerations

Opportunity cost analysis must also consider time commitments and liquidity differences between alternative investments, as less liquid investments might require return premiums to compensate for reduced flexibility and increased commitment requirements.

Real estate investments might generate higher returns than stock investments but require greater time commitments, active management, and reduced liquidity that create additional costs and constraints that affect the true opportunity cost calculation beyond simple return comparisons.

These qualitative factors often prove as important as quantitative return differences in determining optimal investment strategies, particularly for investors with limited time availability or specific liquidity requirements that constrain investment alternatives.

Strategic Opportunity Cost Applications

Understanding opportunity cost enables strategic thinking about portfolio construction, career decisions, and life choices that affect wealth-building potential while providing frameworks for optimizing resource allocation across competing priorities and objectives.

Capital Allocation Optimization

Portfolio-level opportunity cost analysis ensures that capital allocation decisions consider the marginal returns available from increasing allocations to existing investments versus deploying capital in new investment categories or opportunities.

This analysis might reveal that increasing allocations to underperforming asset classes provides better risk-adjusted returns than continuing to invest in currently successful categories that might be becoming overvalued or overcrowded with capital.

Dynamic rebalancing strategies based on opportunity cost analysis can enhance portfolio returns by systematically shifting capital toward investments offering the most attractive risk-adjusted return potential relative to current portfolio holdings and market alternatives.

Career and Education Investment Decisions

Opportunity cost principles apply to human capital investments such as education and career development, where time and money invested in skill development must generate returns that exceed alternative uses for the same resources.

Graduate education decisions, professional certification programs, and career change considerations all involve opportunity costs that should be evaluated systematically using projection frameworks similar to those applied to financial investments.

The returns from human capital investments often exceed financial investment returns over long time horizons while providing diversification benefits and inflation protection that enhance overall wealth-building strategies when properly integrated with financial investment planning.

Growth Forecasting: Predicting Future Performance

Growth forecasting represents the most challenging yet essential component of investment projection, requiring systematic approaches to predicting future performance based on historical patterns, current conditions, and reasonable assumptions about economic and business evolution over time.

Effective growth forecasting balances optimistic potential with realistic constraints while incorporating multiple scenarios that reflect the inherent uncertainty in all future predictions. This balanced approach enables informed decision-making without creating false precision about inherently unpredictable future events.

Understanding different forecasting methodologies and their appropriate applications enables more sophisticated investment analysis while avoiding common mistakes that lead to overconfidence in projections or inadequate consideration of alternative outcomes that could significantly affect investment results.

Historical Analysis and Trend Projection

Historical analysis provides the foundation for most growth forecasting by revealing patterns, cycles, and relationships that might continue into the future while highlighting factors that have driven past performance and might influence future outcomes.

Trend Analysis and Extrapolation

Simple trend analysis examines historical growth patterns to identify consistent trajectories that might continue under similar conditions, providing baseline projections that can be modified based on changing circumstances and expected developments.

Linear trend analysis assumes constant growth rates that extend historical averages into the future, while exponential trend analysis incorporates compound growth patterns that might be more appropriate for businesses or investments exhibiting consistent percentage growth rather than absolute dollar growth.

However, trend extrapolation must be applied cautiously, as historical patterns might not continue due to changing competitive conditions, economic environments, or business life cycles that could dramatically alter future growth trajectories from historical experience.

Cyclical Pattern Recognition

Many investments exhibit cyclical patterns related to economic cycles, industry development phases, or seasonal factors that create predictable fluctuations around long-term growth trends while providing timing insights for strategic positioning.

Understanding these cycles enables more sophisticated forecasting that anticipates periods of above-trend and below-trend performance while avoiding the mistake of extrapolating temporary cyclical peaks or troughs as permanent changes in long-term growth potential.

Cyclical analysis also provides risk management insights by highlighting periods when investments might be vulnerable to downturns or positioned for recovery, enabling strategic timing decisions that enhance return potential while reducing risk exposure.

Fundamental Analysis and Growth Drivers

Fundamental analysis examines the underlying factors that drive investment performance, enabling more sophisticated growth forecasting based on business quality, competitive advantages, market opportunities, and management effectiveness rather than purely statistical extrapolation.

Business Quality Assessment

High-quality businesses typically demonstrate more predictable and sustainable growth patterns than lower-quality alternatives, enabling more confident long-term projections while reducing the risk of dramatic performance deterioration that could invalidate growth assumptions.

Quality indicators include competitive advantages, market positions, financial strength, management quality, and operational efficiency that support sustainable growth over extended periods while providing resilience during challenging economic conditions.

Assessing business quality requires understanding industry dynamics, competitive landscapes, and strategic positioning that determine whether companies can maintain or improve their market positions while defending against competitive threats and capitalizing on growth opportunities.

Market Opportunity Analysis

Growth forecasting must consider the size and growth potential of markets in which investments operate, as even excellent companies cannot exceed the growth limitations imposed by their addressable markets over extended periods.

Market analysis examines factors such as population growth, demographic trends, technological adoption, regulatory changes, and economic development that drive demand for products and services while creating opportunities for business expansion.

Understanding market dynamics also reveals potential constraints on growth, such as market saturation, competitive intensification, or technological disruption that could limit future expansion regardless of company quality or strategic execution.

Scenario Analysis and Probability Weighting

Sophisticated growth forecasting incorporates multiple scenarios with different probability weightings rather than relying on single-point estimates that cannot capture the range of potential outcomes or their likelihood of occurrence.

Multiple Scenario Development

Effective scenario analysis typically includes optimistic, pessimistic, and base-case scenarios that reflect different combinations of assumptions about key variables affecting investment performance while providing range estimates for potential outcomes.

Optimistic scenarios might assume favorable economic conditions, successful strategy execution, and positive competitive developments, while pessimistic scenarios incorporate economic downturns, execution failures, or adverse competitive changes that could impair performance.

Base-case scenarios represent most likely outcomes based on reasonable assumptions about normal business conditions and average performance levels, providing realistic expectations that can guide strategic planning and risk management decisions.

Probability Assessment and Weighting

Assigning probability weights to different scenarios enables calculation of expected values that incorporate both potential outcomes and their likelihood, providing more sophisticated projections than simple averages of scenario results.

Probability assessment requires considering factors such as historical precedent, current conditions, management quality, competitive positioning, and economic indicators that affect the likelihood of different scenario outcomes.

Expected value calculations multiply scenario outcomes by their probability weights and sum the results, creating composite projections that reflect both optimistic potential and pessimistic risks while providing realistic expectations for investment planning purposes.

Strategic Decision-Making Frameworks

Strategic decision-making frameworks transform investment projections into actionable strategies by providing systematic approaches to evaluating opportunities, timing decisions, and managing portfolios that align with personal goals and risk tolerance levels.

These frameworks integrate quantitative projections with qualitative factors and personal circumstances to create comprehensive decision-making processes that optimize investment selection and timing while maintaining discipline during periods of market volatility or emotional pressure.

Effective decision-making frameworks also provide accountability mechanisms and review processes that enable continuous improvement and adaptation based on changing circumstances and lessons learned from investment experience.

Multi-Criteria Decision Analysis

Multi-criteria decision analysis provides systematic approaches to evaluating investments across multiple dimensions simultaneously, ensuring that decisions consider all relevant factors rather than focusing narrowly on single metrics or characteristics.

Weighted Scoring Systems

Weighted scoring systems assign numerical ratings to different investment criteria based on their importance and performance levels, creating composite scores that enable objective comparison across diverse investment opportunities with different characteristics.

Common criteria might include expected return potential, risk levels, liquidity requirements, time commitments, complexity levels, and alignment with personal values or expertise areas that affect investment attractiveness and implementation success.

Weighting factors reflect personal priorities and circumstances, enabling customization of scoring systems to individual needs while maintaining systematic approaches to opportunity evaluation that reduce emotional bias and improve decision consistency.

Decision Trees and Sequential Analysis

Decision tree analysis maps out sequential decision points and their potential outcomes, enabling systematic evaluation of complex investment strategies that involve multiple stages or contingent decisions based on future developments.

This approach proves particularly valuable for investments involving options, such as real estate development projects, business acquisitions, or growth stock investments where future expansion decisions depend on initial results and changing market conditions.

Sequential analysis also reveals the value of maintaining flexibility and avoiding premature commitments that might prevent optimal responses to changing circumstances or new information that emerges during investment holding periods.

Portfolio Integration and Optimization

Individual investment decisions must be evaluated within the context of broader portfolio objectives and constraints, ensuring that new investments enhance overall portfolio performance while maintaining appropriate diversification and risk management.

Correlation Analysis and Diversification

Understanding correlation relationships between potential investments and existing portfolio holdings prevents excessive concentration risks while identifying opportunities for genuine diversification that reduces overall portfolio volatility without sacrificing return potential.

Correlation analysis examines how different investments tend to move relative to each other during various market conditions, enabling portfolio construction that balances growth potential with stability through strategic combination of assets with different performance patterns.

Effective diversification requires understanding not just historical correlations but the fundamental factors that drive investment performance, as correlations can change during market stress periods when diversification benefits are most needed.

Dynamic Allocation and Rebalancing

Portfolio optimization frameworks provide systematic approaches to capital allocation and rebalancing that maintain desired risk-return profiles while adapting to changing market conditions and investment opportunities.

Target allocation strategies specify desired percentage allocations to different asset classes or investment categories, providing discipline for systematic rebalancing that maintains portfolio balance while capturing opportunities created by market fluctuations.

Dynamic allocation strategies adjust target allocations based on market valuations, economic conditions, or personal circumstances that affect optimal portfolio positioning, enabling tactical adjustments within strategic frameworks that maintain long-term focus.

Personal Goal Alignment: Making Numbers Meaningful

Investment projections become truly powerful when aligned with specific personal goals and life objectives, transforming abstract calculations into meaningful planning tools that guide strategic decision-making and motivate disciplined execution over extended periods.

Goal alignment requires understanding both the quantitative requirements for achieving specific objectives and the qualitative factors that determine success, including behavioral requirements, time commitments, and lifestyle implications that affect implementation success.

This alignment process also provides accountability frameworks and progress measurement systems that enable course corrections and strategic adjustments while maintaining focus on ultimate objectives rather than short-term market fluctuations or performance variations.

Quantifying Personal Financial Goals

Transforming vague financial aspirations into specific, measurable objectives enables systematic planning and progress tracking while providing clear targets that guide investment strategy selection and implementation priorities.

SMART Goal Framework Application

SMART goals are Specific, Measurable, Achievable, Relevant, and Time-bound, providing frameworks for converting general financial aspirations into concrete objectives that can be systematically pursued through disciplined investment strategies.

For example, "building wealth for retirement" becomes "accumulating $2 million in retirement accounts by age 65 to generate $80,000 in annual retirement income," providing specific targets that guide investment selection, contribution levels, and strategic planning decisions.

The measurable nature of SMART goals enables regular progress assessment and strategic adjustments while maintaining motivation through clear achievement milestones that demonstrate progress toward ultimate objectives.

Goal Prioritization and Resource Allocation

Multiple financial goals require prioritization and resource allocation decisions that optimize progress across competing objectives while ensuring that essential goals receive adequate resources and attention within available constraints.

Priority assessment considers factors such as time sensitivity, achievement difficulty, opportunity costs, and personal importance that determine optimal resource allocation among different goals while maintaining balanced progress toward multiple objectives.

Resource allocation frameworks enable systematic capital deployment that maximizes overall goal achievement while maintaining flexibility to adjust priorities based on changing circumstances, unexpected opportunities, or shifting personal preferences over time.

Implementation Strategy Development

Effective goal achievement requires implementation strategies that translate quantitative projections into specific action plans with clear timelines, responsibilities, and accountability mechanisms that support disciplined execution.

Action Plan Creation

Implementation strategies specify the specific investments, contribution levels, timing decisions, and management activities required to achieve projected outcomes while identifying potential obstacles and contingency plans that address implementation challenges.

Action plans include specific timelines with milestone targets that enable progress tracking and course correction while breaking large goals into manageable components that maintain motivation and momentum through systematic achievement of intermediate objectives.

Regular review and update processes ensure that implementation strategies remain aligned with changing circumstances and market conditions while maintaining focus on ultimate objectives and adapting tactics as needed to optimize goal achievement probability.

Progress Monitoring and Adjustment Systems

Systematic monitoring systems track actual progress against projected timelines and outcomes, enabling early identification of performance gaps or strategic opportunities that require implementation adjustments or goal modifications.

Key performance indicators provide objective measures of implementation success while highlighting areas requiring additional attention or strategic modification to maintain progress toward ultimate objectives within acceptable risk parameters.

Adjustment protocols specify criteria and procedures for making strategic changes while maintaining accountability for goal achievement and preventing emotional decision-making that could undermine long-term success through reactive responses to short-term performance variations.

Your Investment Projection Action Plan

Mastering investment projection requires systematic skill development combined with practical application across various investment scenarios and market conditions, building competency through structured learning and implementation phases that enhance analytical capabilities over time.

Your projection education should progress from basic mathematical understanding through sophisticated strategic applications that integrate quantitative analysis with qualitative insights and personal goal alignment for comprehensive investment planning.

Building projection expertise represents a long-term commitment requiring patience and consistent practice while maintaining awareness of projection limitations and the inherent uncertainty in all investment endeavors.

Phase 1: Foundation Building (Months 1-2)

Mathematical Foundation Development

Begin your projection education by mastering time value of money calculations, ROI analysis, and basic forecasting techniques through systematic study and practical application to real investment scenarios that build confidence with essential mathematical tools.

Practice manual calculations using financial calculators or spreadsheet software to ensure complete understanding of underlying mathematical relationships while building familiarity with different calculation methods and their appropriate applications.

Create personal reference materials that summarize key formulas, calculation methods, and interpretation guidelines for different projection techniques, providing quick access to essential information during actual analysis situations.

Historical Analysis Skills

Develop proficiency in historical data analysis and trend identification through examination of various investment types across different time periods and market conditions, building pattern recognition capabilities that support effective forecasting.

Study historical examples of successful and unsuccessful investments across different categories to understand the factors that drive performance variations while building intuitive understanding of realistic return expectations and risk characteristics.

Practice trend analysis and cyclical pattern recognition using historical data to develop skills in identifying sustainable patterns versus temporary anomalies that might mislead projection efforts.

Phase 2: Strategic Application Development (Months 3-4)

Goal Integration and Planning

Apply projection skills to personal financial goals by developing specific, measurable objectives that can be systematically pursued through strategic investment planning while maintaining motivation through clear achievement targets.

Create comprehensive financial plans that integrate multiple goals with appropriate priority rankings and resource allocation strategies, ensuring that projection work serves practical planning purposes rather than purely academic exercises.

Practice scenario analysis and contingency planning to develop skills in managing uncertainty while maintaining progress toward objectives despite changing conditions or unexpected developments.

Advanced Projection Techniques

Develop proficiency with sophisticated forecasting methods including fundamental analysis, scenario modeling, and probability weighting that provide more accurate and realistic projections for complex investment decisions.

Learn to integrate quantitative projections with qualitative factors such as management quality, competitive advantages, and market dynamics that significantly affect investment outcomes but might not be captured in purely numerical analysis.

Practice portfolio-level optimization and strategic decision-making that considers projection results within broader investment frameworks rather than as isolated analytical exercises.

Phase 3: Implementation and Refinement (Months 5-6)

Real-World Application

Begin applying projection skills to actual investment decisions with appropriate risk management and position sizing that enables learning while limiting potential losses during skill development phases.

Document projection assumptions and methodologies to enable performance evaluation and continuous improvement based on actual outcomes versus projected results, building calibration skills that enhance future projection accuracy.

Develop systematic review and adjustment processes that enable adaptation based on changing circumstances while maintaining accountability for goal achievement and strategic consistency.

Strategic Integration

Build comprehensive investment management systems that integrate projection capabilities with portfolio management, risk control, and goal achievement tracking for effective wealth-building implementation.

Create decision-making frameworks that balance projection results with other factors such as risk tolerance, time availability, and personal preferences to optimize investment strategies for individual circumstances and objectives.

Establish networks with other analytical investors for perspective sharing and methodology discussion while maintaining independent analytical thinking that supports confident decision-making based on personal projection work.

The Projection Advantage That Transforms Your Financial Future

As we conclude this comprehensive exploration of investment value projection, remember that you now possess analytical capabilities that distinguish strategic investors from reactive participants who make decisions based on hope, emotion, or incomplete analysis. Your ability to project outcomes, evaluate opportunities, and align investments with goals provides substantial advantages in building wealth systematically over time.

The projection skills you develop through systematic application of these frameworks compound over time, becoming more valuable as your experience grows and pattern recognition capabilities mature through exposure to various market conditions and investment scenarios. These analytical advantages provide lasting competitive benefits that support superior investment results.

Your journey toward projection mastery requires dedication to continuous learning and skill refinement while maintaining realistic expectations about projection limitations and the inherent uncertainty in all investment endeavors. The most successful projectionists balance analytical rigor with appropriate humility about prediction accuracy while using projections as tools for improved decision-making rather than guarantees of future outcomes.

The investment opportunities that once seemed overwhelming or unpredictable now serve as analytical challenges where your projection capabilities provide clarity and confidence in strategic decision-making that aligns with your most important life objectives.

Chapter Challenge: Build Your Projection Capabilities

This Week:

- Master basic ROI calculations and time value of money concepts through practical application to real investment examples

- Define 3-5 specific financial goals using SMART goal frameworks with quantitative targets and timelines

- Begin tracking historical performance data for investment categories that interest you most

- Practice basic forecasting techniques using historical data to project future growth potential

This Month:

- Develop comprehensive projection models for your primary financial goals with multiple scenario analysis

- Apply opportunity cost analysis to current investment decisions and potential alternatives

- Create systematic decision-making frameworks that integrate projection results with personal preferences and constraints

- Begin documenting projection assumptions and methodologies for future performance evaluation

This Quarter:

- Implement investment strategies based on projection work with appropriate risk management and position sizing

- Refine projection techniques based on practical application results and changing market conditions

- Build comprehensive financial planning systems that integrate all projection capabilities with goal achievement tracking

- Establish regular review processes that enable continuous improvement and strategic adaptation based on experience

Remember that projection excellence develops through patient application of systematic approaches combined with continuous learning and adaptation based on actual outcomes and changing circumstances. The most successful projectionists treat their analytical work as ongoing disciplines requiring constant refinement rather than one-time exercises that provide permanent answers.

Your wealth rebellion continues with every projection you complete based on evidence rather than hope, every strategic decision guided by analytical frameworks rather than emotion, and every goal achieved through systematic planning rather than luck or chance. The projection capabilities you develop provide lasting advantages that compound throughout your wealth-building journey.

In our next chapter, we will explore advanced techniques for building wealth with minimal financial investment, demonstrating how creativity, knowledge, and strategic thinking can create substantial value even when capital resources are limited, opening pathways to financial success that don't require significant initial investment.

The future belongs to those who can see it clearly through systematic analysis and strategic projection. Your commitment to projection excellence begins with recognizing that informed strategic planning based on realistic analysis provides significant advantages over reactive decision-making or wishful thinking about investment outcomes that ignore mathematical reality and market constraints.

Chapter 17: Achieving Financial Independence

"Financial independence is not a distant dream reserved for the fortunate few—it is a destination accessible to anyone willing to embark upon the disciplined journey of intentional living, strategic planning, and unwavering commitment to their future self. It represents the ultimate expression of personal sovereignty, where your choices are guided by your values rather than constrained by your bank balance."

We are entering the culminating chapter of your wealth rebellion journey—a sacred space where dreams transform into reality and where the principles you've absorbed throughout this book converge into the magnificent achievement of true financial independence. Here, within these pages, we celebrate not just the destination but the profound transformation that occurs within those who dare to take complete control of their financial destiny.

As we embark upon this final exploration together, I invite you to embrace this knowledge with the heart of a victor and the wisdom of someone who understands that financial independence represents far more than numbers in bank accounts. It embodies the freedom to live according to your deepest values, the power to make choices based on passion rather than paycheck, and the profound peace that comes from knowing you have created security not just for yourself, but for those you love.

This chapter serves as your comprehensive guide to understanding, planning for, and ultimately achieving the financial independence that transforms from distant aspiration into present reality. Together, we will explore what true financial independence means in practical terms, outline the concrete steps that bridge the gap between where you are and where you want to be, and provide the motivational foundation that sustains you through every challenge and celebrates every victory along this extraordinary journey.

Understanding Financial Independence: Your Liberation Defined

Financial independence transcends simple wealth accumulation, representing a state of economic self-sufficiency where your passive income streams and accumulated assets provide complete freedom from dependence on traditional employment or external financial support. This achievement creates the foundation for living life on your own terms while pursuing your highest purposes without constraint from financial limitations.

True financial independence encompasses multiple dimensions including income replacement through investment returns, asset diversification that provides security across various economic conditions, and lifestyle sustainability that maintains desired living standards without depleting principal assets over extended periods.

Understanding this concept requires recognizing that financial independence represents a spectrum rather than a binary state, with various levels of achievement that provide increasing degrees of freedom and security while enabling different lifestyle choices and risk tolerances based on individual priorities and circumstances.

The Anatomy of Financial Freedom

Financial independence operates through the fundamental principle that your accumulated assets generate sufficient passive income to cover all living expenses indefinitely, creating sustainable financial security that doesn't require active work or employment income to maintain desired lifestyle standards.

This mathematical foundation typically requires accumulating assets worth 25-30 times annual expenses, enabling withdrawal rates of 3-4% annually that can theoretically sustain spending levels indefinitely through investment returns while preserving principal value across various market conditions and economic cycles.

However, true financial independence extends beyond mathematical calculations to encompass psychological security, lifestyle flexibility, and the profound sense of empowerment that comes from knowing you possess complete control over your time, energy, and life choices without external financial pressures or constraints.

The Four Pillars of Financial Independence

The first pillar involves income optimization through career development, business ownership, or other strategies that maximize earning potential while building skills and assets that provide ongoing value creation and financial security throughout changing economic conditions and market environments.

Asset accumulation forms the second pillar, requiring systematic investment strategies that build wealth through compound growth while maintaining appropriate diversification and risk management that protects accumulated resources from market volatility and economic uncertainty.

The third pillar encompasses expense optimization through mindful spending that aligns resources with values while eliminating wasteful consumption that doesn't contribute to happiness or well-being, creating sustainable lifestyle patterns that support long-term financial independence goals.

Passive income generation represents the fourth pillar, involving the development of investment portfolios, business systems, or other assets that produce ongoing cash flows without requiring active management, creating the sustainable income streams that ultimately enable true financial independence.

Different Levels of Financial Achievement

Financial security represents the foundational level where you possess sufficient emergency funds and stable income to handle unexpected expenses and economic disruptions without compromising basic living standards or accumulating debt that threatens financial stability.

Financial stability builds upon security by creating predictable income streams and expense patterns that enable consistent progress toward long-term goals while maintaining comfortable living standards and the ability to handle normal life transitions and economic fluctuations.

Financial independence represents full liberation from dependence on employment income, where passive income streams and accumulated assets provide complete financial security while enabling lifestyle choices based on personal preferences rather than economic necessity or external constraints.

Coast Financial Independence

Coast FI represents a milestone where you've accumulated sufficient assets that compound growth alone will provide full financial independence by traditional retirement age, even without additional contributions, creating flexibility to pursue lower-paying but more fulfilling work or take career risks without jeopardizing long-term security.

This achievement typically occurs when someone in their twenties or thirties has accumulated 10-15 times their annual expenses in retirement accounts, enabling the power of compound growth to build full financial independence over 20-30 year periods without requiring additional savings.

Coast FI provides psychological benefits including reduced financial stress and increased career flexibility while maintaining progress toward full financial independence through continued saving and investment that can accelerate timeline achievement and provide additional security margins.

Lean vs. Fat Financial Independence

Lean FI involves achieving financial independence with minimal expense levels, often requiring lifestyle optimization and geographic arbitrage that enables independence on smaller asset bases while maintaining fulfilling but resource-efficient living standards.

This approach appeals to those who prioritize time freedom over luxury consumption, often achieving independence with $500,000-$1,000,000 in assets through careful expense management and lifestyle design that maximizes happiness while minimizing financial requirements.

Fat FI involves accumulating larger asset bases that support higher expense levels and lifestyle standards, typically requiring $2,000,000-$5,000,000 or more in assets while providing greater financial security and lifestyle flexibility without requiring significant expense management or lifestyle constraints.

The Strategic Framework: Your Roadmap to Independence

Achieving financial independence requires systematic approaches that integrate multiple wealth-building strategies while maintaining focus on long-term objectives through disciplined execution and adaptive planning that responds to changing circumstances and opportunities.

This framework operates through interconnected components including income optimization, expense management, investment strategy, and ongoing monitoring that work together to accelerate progress while maintaining sustainability and risk management throughout the journey toward financial independence.

Understanding this framework enables strategic decision-making that optimizes resource allocation and timeline achievement while avoiding common mistakes that can derail progress or compromise long-term financial security through poor planning or execution.

Income Maximization Strategies

Career development represents the most direct path to income growth through skill development, strategic job changes, and performance optimization that commands higher compensation while building valuable expertise and professional networks that support ongoing advancement.

Successful income maximization requires understanding market demand for your skills while continuously developing capabilities that remain valuable across changing economic conditions and technological developments that could affect career prospects and earning potential.

Strategic career management includes networking, continuing education, certification development, and geographic flexibility that positions you advantageously in competitive job markets while building skills and relationships that support sustained income growth over extended periods.

Entrepreneurship and Business Development

Business ownership provides unlimited income potential through value creation that scales beyond time-for-money exchanges, enabling wealth building through both current income and asset appreciation that can accelerate financial independence achievement.

Successful entrepreneurship requires identifying market opportunities where you can create genuine value while building systems and processes that enable scaling without proportional time increases, creating businesses that ultimately operate independently of your direct involvement.

Business development should consider your skills, interests, and market opportunities while maintaining appropriate risk management that doesn't jeopardize existing financial security during the uncertain period when new ventures are being developed and refined.

Multiple Income Stream Development

Diversified income sources provide security against economic downturns or career disruptions while creating opportunities for accelerated wealth building through complementary activities that leverage your skills and resources across multiple domains.

These streams might include employment income, business profits, investment returns, rental income, royalties, or consulting fees that together create robust financial foundations that can withstand disruptions to individual income sources.

Developing multiple streams requires strategic thinking about time allocation and skill development that builds complementary capabilities while avoiding over-diversification that prevents achieving excellence in any particular area or income source.

Investment Strategy and Asset Building

Systematic investment strategies form the foundation of long-term wealth building through compound growth that transforms regular contributions into substantial asset accumulation over extended periods while maintaining appropriate risk management and diversification.

Effective investment strategies balance growth potential with risk management through diversified portfolios that participate in market appreciation while protecting against significant losses that could jeopardize financial independence timelines or retirement security.

Understanding investment principles enables informed decision-making about asset allocation, risk tolerance, and strategic rebalancing that optimizes returns while maintaining appropriate risk levels for your age, circumstances, and financial objectives throughout changing market conditions.

The Power of Compound Interest

Compound growth represents the most powerful force in wealth building, where investment returns generate additional returns that accelerate asset accumulation exponentially over time, creating dramatic differences in final outcomes based on starting age and contribution consistency.

A 25-year-old investing $500 monthly at 8% annual returns accumulates over $1.7 million by age 65, while someone starting at 35 accumulates only $745,000 despite identical contributions, demonstrating the extraordinary value of early start dates and consistent investing.

Understanding compound growth motivates early action while highlighting the importance of consistent contributions and long-term patience that enables maximum benefit from this mathematical phenomenon that transforms modest savings into substantial wealth over time.

Asset Allocation and Diversification

Strategic asset allocation balances growth-oriented investments with stability-focused assets based on your age, risk tolerance, and timeline to financial independence, creating portfolios that optimize expected returns while managing downside risks.

Diversification across asset classes, geographic regions, and investment styles reduces portfolio volatility while maintaining growth potential through exposure to different economic factors and market conditions that affect various investments differently over time.

Effective allocation strategies evolve with changing circumstances and market conditions while maintaining discipline during volatile periods when emotional responses might compromise long-term strategy effectiveness and wealth-building progress.

Passive Income Development

Passive income streams provide the foundation for financial independence through assets that generate ongoing cash flows without requiring active management, creating sustainable income that can replace employment earnings while preserving accumulated wealth.

Building passive income requires initial capital investment and often significant upfront effort to establish systems that subsequently operate with minimal ongoing involvement, creating assets that appreciate while providing income throughout the wealth-building journey.

Understanding different passive income opportunities enables strategic selection based on your interests, skills, and available resources while building diversified income streams that provide security and flexibility throughout your financial independence journey.

Dividend Investing and REIT Strategies

Dividend-paying stocks and Real Estate Investment Trusts provide regular income payments while offering potential for capital appreciation, creating dual benefits that support both current cash flow needs and long-term wealth accumulation objectives.

High-quality dividend stocks from established companies often provide reliable income streams that grow over time through dividend increases, creating inflation-adjusted income that becomes increasingly valuable during financial independence phases.

REIT investments provide real estate exposure through liquid securities that distribute most earnings as dividends, enabling real estate investment benefits without direct property management responsibilities while maintaining portfolio liquidity and diversification.

Real Estate Investment Opportunities

Direct real estate investment through rental properties can provide substantial passive income while building equity through property appreciation and mortgage paydown, creating wealth through multiple simultaneous mechanisms that accelerate financial independence achievement.

Successful real estate investing requires understanding local markets, property management systems, and financial analysis that ensures positive cash flow while building long-term wealth through appreciation and debt reduction over extended holding periods.

Real estate investment platforms and crowdfunding opportunities enable participation in real estate markets with lower capital requirements and reduced management responsibilities while providing exposure to professional real estate development and management expertise.

Budgeting Mastery: Your Financial Foundation

Effective budgeting provides the foundation for all wealth-building activities by creating systematic approaches to income and expense management that maximize resources available for saving and investment while maintaining sustainable lifestyle patterns that support long-term financial goals.

Budgeting mastery involves understanding cash flow patterns, identifying optimization opportunities, and implementing systems that balance current lifestyle needs with future financial security through disciplined resource allocation and strategic spending decisions.

This discipline enables acceleration of financial independence timelines through increased savings rates while maintaining quality of life and personal satisfaction that makes the wealth-building journey sustainable and enjoyable rather than restrictive or punitive.

The Science of Expense Tracking

Systematic expense tracking reveals spending patterns and identifies optimization opportunities that might not be apparent without detailed analysis of where money actually goes versus where you intend to allocate resources for various needs and priorities.

Modern tracking tools enable automatic categorization and analysis that reduces administrative burden while providing insights into spending trends that inform strategic budget adjustments and lifestyle optimization decisions that support accelerated wealth building.

Effective tracking balances detail with simplicity, providing sufficient information for informed decision-making without creating administrative burdens that compromise system sustainability or become obstacles to consistent implementation and ongoing use.

Identifying Spending Leaks

Small recurring expenses often accumulate into substantial annual costs that represent significant opportunities for savings redirection toward wealth-building activities without meaningfully impacting lifestyle quality or personal satisfaction.

Common spending leaks include subscription services that aren't actively used, convenience purchases that could be eliminated through better planning, and lifestyle inflation that increases expenses without corresponding increases in happiness or life satisfaction.

Systematic leak identification involves reviewing all recurring expenses and evaluating their contribution to your values and goals while eliminating or optimizing costs that don't provide commensurate value or support your financial independence objectives.

Value-Based Spending Alignment

Strategic spending aligns resource allocation with personal values and priorities while eliminating expenses that don't contribute to happiness, goals, or life satisfaction, creating spending patterns that support both current well-being and long-term financial objectives.

This alignment involves understanding what purchases and experiences provide genuine value while identifying areas where spending reductions wouldn't meaningfully impact quality of life but could significantly accelerate wealth-building progress.

Value-based spending enables sustainable budgeting that doesn't feel restrictive because resources are directed toward things you genuinely care about while eliminating waste that doesn't serve your priorities or contribute to your overall life satisfaction.

Strategic Budget Optimization

Budget optimization involves systematic analysis of spending categories to identify opportunities for cost reduction without lifestyle compromise while redirecting saved resources toward wealth-building activities that accelerate financial independence achievement.

This process requires understanding fixed versus variable expenses, identifying negotiation opportunities, and implementing strategic changes that reduce costs while maintaining or improving service quality and life satisfaction through more efficient resource utilization.

Optimization should be viewed as an ongoing process rather than a one-time activity, with regular reviews that identify new opportunities while adapting to changing circumstances and priorities that affect optimal resource allocation strategies.

Fixed Expense Reduction Strategies

Housing costs typically represent the largest expense category, making optimization through location choices, housing type decisions, or refinancing opportunities potentially significant for accelerated savings without proportional lifestyle impact.

Transportation optimization through vehicle choices, maintenance strategies, and commuting decisions can provide substantial savings while potentially improving rather than compromising quality of life through reduced commuting stress or improved vehicle reliability.

Insurance, utilities, and communication services offer optimization opportunities through provider comparison, plan adjustment, and bundling strategies that reduce costs while maintaining or improving service quality and coverage levels.

Variable Expense Management

Food and dining expenses provide significant optimization opportunities through meal planning, cooking skills development, and strategic dining choices that can reduce costs while potentially improving nutrition and social experiences.

Entertainment and recreation optimization involves finding cost-effective activities that provide equal or greater enjoyment while redirecting resources toward wealth building that ultimately provides greater long-term satisfaction and security.

Shopping and consumption optimization requires strategic timing, quality focus, and needs-versus-wants analysis that reduces unnecessary purchases while ensuring that needed items are acquired efficiently and cost-effectively.

Building Unstoppable Momentum: Motivation for the Journey

Financial independence journeys require sustained motivation over extended periods that can span decades, making psychological sustainability as important as mathematical strategy for successful achievement of long-term wealth-building objectives.

Understanding motivation psychology enables development of systems and mindsets that maintain enthusiasm and discipline through inevitable challenges, setbacks, and temptations that test commitment to long-term goals throughout the wealth-building process.

Building unstoppable momentum involves creating positive feedback loops, celebrating progress milestones, and maintaining connection with deeper purposes that make financial independence meaningful beyond simple number achievement or external recognition.

The Psychology of Long-Term Success

Long-term financial success requires developing delayed gratification capabilities that prioritize future benefits over immediate pleasures while maintaining enough present-moment satisfaction to make the journey sustainable and personally fulfilling.

This balance involves understanding your psychological triggers and developing systems that support consistent decision-making aligned with long-term objectives while avoiding deprivation that could lead to unsustainable restriction or eventual abandonment of wealth-building goals.

Successful long-term thinking involves regular visualization of future benefits, connection with deeper purposes, and systematic reinforcement of decisions that support wealth-building objectives through progress tracking and milestone celebration.

Overcoming Instant Gratification Culture

Modern consumer culture constantly promotes immediate satisfaction through spending and consumption that conflicts with wealth-building discipline, requiring conscious resistance to marketing messages and social pressures that encourage short-term thinking.

Developing resistance involves understanding marketing psychology, building decision-making frameworks that consider long-term costs and benefits, and creating environments that support wealth-building decisions while minimizing exposure to consumption temptations.

Alternative satisfaction strategies include focusing on experiences over possessions, finding community among like-minded individuals, and developing hobbies and interests that provide fulfillment without significant financial cost or consumption requirements.

Creating Positive Feedback Loops

Regular progress tracking provides positive reinforcement that maintains motivation through visible evidence of advancement toward financial independence goals while creating satisfaction from systematic achievement and discipline.

Milestone celebrations acknowledge significant achievements while providing motivation to continue progressing toward ultimate objectives through recognition of effort and progress that might not be immediately visible in daily activities.

Community engagement with others pursuing similar goals provides support, accountability, and shared learning that makes the journey more enjoyable while providing encouragement during challenging periods and celebration during successful phases.

Milestone Celebration and Progress Tracking

Systematic progress tracking transforms abstract long-term goals into concrete achievements that provide ongoing motivation while enabling strategic adjustments that optimize progress and maintain momentum throughout the financial independence journey.

Effective tracking systems balance detail with simplicity while providing clear visibility into progress across multiple dimensions including net worth growth, savings rate improvement, and passive income development that collectively contribute to financial independence achievement.

Celebration strategies acknowledge both major milestones and consistent effort, recognizing that long-term success results from accumulated daily decisions and discipline rather than occasional dramatic achievements or breakthrough moments.

Net Worth Milestones and Significance

Net worth milestones provide concrete measures of progress that enable celebration and motivation while serving as checkpoints for strategy evaluation and adjustment based on actual results versus projected timelines and expectations.

Significant milestones might include reaching positive net worth, achieving specific dollar amounts, or accumulating sufficient assets to support various levels of financial independence that provide increasing degrees of freedom and security.

Milestone achievement should be balanced with ongoing focus on process and systems that create sustainable progress rather than becoming obsessed with numbers that might create anxiety or compromise long-term strategy effectiveness.

Savings Rate Achievement and Optimization

Savings rate represents one of the most powerful factors determining financial independence timeline, making savings rate improvement a crucial focus area that provides immediate feedback on progress and optimization effectiveness.

High savings rates require both income optimization and expense management while maintaining lifestyle sustainability that enables long-term adherence to wealth-building strategies without creating unsustainable restriction or lifestyle compromise.

Savings rate tracking enables experimentation with different strategies while providing clear feedback on effectiveness that informs ongoing optimization and strategic adjustment based on actual results and personal satisfaction levels.

Sustaining Motivation Through Challenges

Financial independence journeys inevitably include market downturns, career setbacks, and personal challenges that test commitment while potentially creating discouragement or temptation to abandon long-term strategies in favor of short-term relief.

Building resilience involves preparing mentally and strategically for challenges while developing coping strategies that maintain long-term focus during difficult periods when progress might stall or temporary setbacks might threaten accumulated wealth.

Sustainable motivation systems provide support during challenging periods while maintaining connection with deeper purposes and long-term benefits that make temporary sacrifice and discipline worthwhile for ultimate achievement and security.

Market Volatility and Emotional Management

Investment portfolio volatility creates psychological challenges that can undermine long-term strategy effectiveness if emotional responses lead to market timing attempts or strategy abandonment during periods of market stress or declining values.

Preparing for volatility involves understanding historical market patterns, developing perspective on temporary fluctuations versus long-term trends, and maintaining focus on strategy consistency rather than short-term portfolio value changes.

Emotional management strategies include regular education about market behavior, community support from experienced investors, and systematic approaches to portfolio management that reduce emotional decision-making during stressful market periods.

Life Event Adaptation and Flexibility

Major life changes including career transitions, family developments, or health challenges may require strategy adjustments while maintaining core commitment to financial independence objectives through adaptive planning and flexible implementation.

Building flexibility involves emergency fund maintenance, diversified income sources, and planning frameworks that can accommodate changing circumstances without completely derailing long-term wealth-building progress and achievement.

Adaptation strategies should balance accommodation of new circumstances with maintenance of long-term objectives through strategic adjustments rather than complete strategy abandonment that sacrifices accumulated progress and future security.

Your Personal Financial Independence Action Plan

Creating a personalized action plan transforms financial independence from abstract goal into systematic process with specific steps, timelines, and milestones that guide decision-making while providing structure for consistent progress toward ultimate achievement.

This plan should integrate all wealth-building strategies explored throughout this book while adapting them to your specific circumstances, goals, and resources through realistic assessment and strategic prioritization that optimizes progress within your constraints and opportunities.

Implementation success requires balancing ambitious goal-setting with realistic execution capabilities while creating systems that support consistent progress through changing circumstances and evolving understanding about optimal strategies and approaches.

Phase 1: Foundation Building (Months 1-6)

Initial foundation building involves establishing basic financial systems including emergency funds, debt elimination strategies, and investment account setup that provide platforms for subsequent wealth-building activities and advanced strategy implementation.

This phase emphasizes stability and system establishment rather than aggressive wealth building, ensuring solid foundations that support sustainable long-term progress without creating financial stress or instability during the learning and implementation process.

Foundation building should include financial education, goal clarification, and initial strategy development that prepares you for subsequent phases while building confidence and competency through manageable initial steps and quick wins.

Emergency Fund and Debt Management

Building adequate emergency funds provides financial security that enables investment risk-taking while protecting against life disruptions that could derail wealth-building progress through forced asset liquidation or debt accumulation during challenging periods.

Debt elimination prioritization typically focuses on high-interest debt while maintaining minimum payments on lower-interest obligations, freeing cash flow for wealth-building activities while reducing financial stress and interest expense burdens.

Emergency fund sizing should consider income stability, expense variability, and personal risk tolerance while providing sufficient cushion for major life disruptions without creating excessive cash drag that limits wealth-building potential.

Investment Account Setup and Automation

Investment account establishment includes retirement account optimization, taxable account opening, and automatic contribution systems that ensure consistent wealth building without requiring ongoing decision-making or administrative management.

Account selection should consider tax advantages, investment options, fee structures, and integration capabilities that optimize long-term wealth building while maintaining simplicity and ease of management throughout changing circumstances.

Automation systems include automatic contributions, investment allocation, and rebalancing that maintain strategic consistency while reducing administrative burden and emotional interference with long-term strategy implementation.

Phase 2: Acceleration and Optimization (Months 7-18)

Acceleration phases involve implementing advanced strategies including income optimization, expense management, and sophisticated investment approaches that accelerate progress while building expertise and confidence through practical application and experience.

This phase emphasizes strategy refinement and optimization based on initial results while exploring opportunities for income diversification, advanced tax strategies, and passive income development that support accelerated timeline achievement.

Optimization should include regular strategy review and adjustment based on actual results, changing circumstances, and evolving understanding about effective approaches that provide superior results within your specific situation and constraints.

Income and Expense Optimization

Income optimization might include career advancement strategies, side business development, or skill building that commands higher compensation while creating multiple income streams that provide security and acceleration opportunities.

Expense optimization involves systematic review of all spending categories while implementing strategies that reduce costs without compromising values or life satisfaction through strategic substitution and efficiency improvement.

Optimization balance requires maintaining lifestyle sustainability while maximizing resources available for wealth building through strategic decision-making that considers both short-term satisfaction and long-term financial objectives.

Investment Strategy Refinement

Strategy refinement involves portfolio optimization, asset allocation adjustment, and advanced technique implementation based on experience and changing circumstances while maintaining core strategy consistency and long-term focus.

Investment education should continue throughout this phase through reading, courses, or professional consultation that builds expertise while avoiding over-complexity that might compromise strategy effectiveness or implementation consistency.

Refinement activities include rebalancing optimization, tax-loss harvesting implementation, and account coordination that maximizes efficiency while maintaining appropriate risk management and diversification principles.

Phase 3: Financial Independence Achievement (Months 19+)

Final phases involve implementing sophisticated strategies while monitoring progress toward specific financial independence targets through milestone tracking and strategy adjustment that optimize timeline achievement and post-independence sustainability.

This phase emphasizes sustainability planning, passive income optimization, and transition preparation that ensures smooth movement from accumulation to independence phases while maintaining financial security and lifestyle satisfaction.

Achievement planning should include withdrawal strategy development, healthcare planning, and activity planning that ensures successful transition to financial independence life while maintaining purpose and engagement beyond financial achievement.

Passive Income Optimization

Passive income development involves building diversified income streams through investment dividends, real estate income, business income, or other sources that provide sustainable cash flow without requiring active management or ongoing work.

Income stream diversification reduces dependence on single sources while providing security against economic changes or industry disruptions that might affect specific income types or investment categories.

Optimization strategies include tax efficiency, cash flow timing, and growth potential that maximize income while maintaining principal preservation and inflation protection throughout long-term financial independence periods.

Independence Transition Planning

Transition planning involves developing post-independence activities, maintaining healthcare coverage, and creating lifestyle structures that provide meaning and engagement beyond financial achievement while maintaining social connections and personal growth.

Financial transition includes withdrawal strategy implementation, tax planning optimization, and portfolio management approaches that sustain financial independence while adapting to changing needs and market conditions over extended periods.

Life transition planning considers housing, location, activities, and relationships that create fulfilling independence phases while maintaining flexibility for changing interests, health considerations, and family circumstances that might affect optimal lifestyle choices.

The Dawn of Your Financial Freedom

As we conclude this transformative exploration of financial independence achievement, remember that you now possess comprehensive knowledge and strategic frameworks that can transform your financial future from uncertain dependency into secure independence through disciplined implementation and patient persistence.

The journey toward financial independence represents more than wealth accumulation—it embodies personal development, strategic thinking, and the profound satisfaction that comes from taking complete control of your financial destiny while creating security and opportunities for yourself and those you love.

Your path forward requires commitment to long-term thinking, discipline in daily decisions, and faith in the power of compound growth and systematic progress that transforms modest beginnings into substantial achievement through patient application of proven principles and strategies.

The financial independence that once seemed like an impossible dream now stands before you as an achievable reality, requiring only your commitment to implementation and persistence through the inevitable challenges and opportunities that characterize every successful wealth-building journey.

Chapter Challenge: Launch Your Independence Journey Today

This Week:

- Calculate your specific financial independence number based on desired annual expenses and withdrawal rate assumptions
- Assess your current net worth and savings rate to establish baseline measurements for progress tracking
- Open necessary investment accounts and establish automatic contribution systems that ensure consistent wealth building
- Create detailed budget tracking systems that identify optimization opportunities and monitor progress toward savings rate goals

This Month:

- Develop comprehensive action plan with specific timelines, milestones, and strategies adapted to your circumstances and goals
- Implement initial optimization strategies for both income enhancement and expense reduction that increase savings rate
- Begin systematic investment program with appropriate asset allocation based on age, risk tolerance, and timeline to independence
- Establish progress tracking and milestone celebration systems that maintain motivation throughout your wealth-building journey

This Quarter:

- Evaluate progress against initial goals while refining strategies based on actual results and changing circumstances
- Explore passive income opportunities that align with your interests and resources while supporting long-term independence objectives

- Build communities and relationships that support your financial independence journey through shared learning and accountability

- Develop long-term vision for post-independence life that provides meaning and direction beyond financial achievement alone

Remember that financial independence achievement requires patient persistence over extended periods rather than seeking quick results that might compromise long-term success through unsustainable strategies or unrealistic expectations about timeline achievement.

Your wealth rebellion reaches its ultimate expression through achieving complete financial independence that enables living according to your deepest values while creating security and opportunities that extend far beyond your individual achievement to benefit family members and causes you care about.

The path to financial independence begins with today's decisions and continues through tomorrow's discipline, creating freedom that transforms not just your bank account but your entire approach to living with purpose, security, and unlimited potential for positive impact.

Your journey toward financial independence represents the ultimate victory in your wealth rebellion—proof that individual determination, strategic thinking, and disciplined action can overcome any obstacle while creating the life you've always envisioned for yourself and those you love. The time for action is now, and the destination is freedom.

Chapter 18: You Were Never Broke—Just Uninformed

"The greatest revolution happens not in the streets, but in the mind—when you realize that scarcity was never your reality, only your programming. Today, you shed the skin of the uninformed and emerge as the architect of your own abundance, armed with knowledge that transforms dreams into strategies and strategies into wealth."

Fellow revolutionary, as we reach the culmination of this evolutionary journey together, I invite you to pause and truly absorb the magnitude of what has transpired within these pages. You embarked upon this exploration believing yourself limited by circumstances, constrained by a system that seemed impenetrable, perhaps even convinced that wealth was reserved for others blessed with advantages you did not possess.

But here you stand now, equipped with a treasury of knowledge that illuminates a profound truth: you were never broke—you were simply uninformed. Every financial struggle you faced, every opportunity that seemed beyond reach, every moment you felt excluded from prosperity's inner circle—these experiences were not reflections of your inherent worth or capability, but rather symptoms of information asymmetry that has now been forever remedied.

The system that once appeared to exclude you has revealed its secrets, and you now possess the keys to doors that were always there, merely hidden behind walls of complexity and gatekeepers who profited from your ignorance. Today marks not just the end of a book, but the beginning of your true financial education—a lifelong journey of wealth creation that starts with the fundamental shift in how you see yourself and your place in the economic landscape.

From Consumer to Creator: Your Identity Revolution

Throughout your life, you have been conditioned to see yourself as a consumer—someone whose primary economic function is to purchase products and services created by others, feeding a system that extracts value from your labor while offering limited pathways to true wealth accumulation. This identity has been carefully cultivated by forces that benefit from your consumption and your continued economic dependency.

But within these pages, you have discovered your true identity as a creator—someone capable of generating value, building assets, and constructing wealth through strategic thinking and informed action. You are not merely a participant in the economy; you are a potential architect of it, equipped with the knowledge and tools necessary to flip the traditional script and build lasting prosperity on your own terms.

This transformation from consumer to creator represents more than a simple mindset shift—it embodies a fundamental reorientation of your relationship with money, work, and opportunity. Where you once saw expenses, you now recognize investments. Where you once accepted limitations, you now identify possibilities. Where you once sought jobs, you now envision enterprises. Where you once dreamed of wealth, you now strategize pathways to achieve it.

The Creator's Mindset Revolution

Creators understand that every dollar represents potential energy that can be directed toward wealth-building activities rather than merely consumed for temporary satisfaction. They recognize that time is their most valuable resource, to be invested wisely in activities that compound over time rather than traded hourly for wages that barely sustain them.

You now possess the creator's lens through which every situation becomes an opportunity for value generation. Every problem you encounter represents a potential business solution, every skill you develop becomes a potential income stream, and every connection you make expands your network of possibility for collaborative wealth creation.

The creator's identity encompasses not just entrepreneurship, but strategic thinking about employment, investment, and life choices that align with wealth-building objectives rather than mere survival. You approach career decisions strategically, seeking opportunities that build skills, networks, and equity rather than simply provide paychecks.

From Hustler to Strategist: The Evolution of Effort

Perhaps you entered this journey with the hustler's mentality—believing that success required grinding harder, working longer hours, and outmaneuvering others through sheer determination and relentless effort. While hustle has its place, you have now evolved into something far more powerful: a strategist who understands that sustainable wealth comes not from working harder, but from working smarter.

The hustler relies on personal energy and time, creating wealth that depends entirely on continued effort and presence. The strategist builds systems, acquires assets, and creates multiple income streams that generate wealth even during sleep. The hustler trades time for money; the strategist creates money from ideas, connections, and strategic positioning.

Your transformation from hustler to strategist reflects a sophisticated understanding of leverage—using other people's money, time, expertise, and resources to amplify your efforts and create exponential rather than linear returns on your investments of time, energy, and capital.

Strategic Thinking in Action

Strategists approach opportunities with long-term perspectives, evaluating not just immediate returns but compound effects over time. They understand that the most powerful wealth-building activities may show minimal short-term results while creating substantial long-term value through patient capital appreciation and systematic wealth accumulation.

You now recognize that strategic thinking involves positioning yourself advantageously within systems rather than simply working within them. Instead of accepting market wages, you negotiate based on value creation. Instead of following conventional paths, you identify inefficiencies and opportunities that others overlook.

The strategic mindset encompasses risk management, diversification, and systematic approaches to wealth building that reduce dependence on single income sources while building resilience against economic volatility and changing market conditions that might devastate those who rely solely on hustling.

Wealth Isn't Luck—It's Learning the Game

One of the most liberating realizations from your journey is that wealth creation follows patterns and principles that can be learned, applied, and replicated by anyone willing to invest in their financial education. The mythology of wealth as luck, inheritance, or mysterious talent has been replaced by your understanding of wealth as the natural result of strategic thinking and informed action.

Every wealthy individual you now study reveals similar patterns: they understood money principles that create compound growth, they positioned themselves in appreciating assets rather than depreciating expenses, they built multiple income streams instead of depending on single sources, and they consistently reinvested profits into additional wealth-generating activities.

These patterns are not secrets reserved for the privileged few—they are learnable skills and principles available to anyone willing to study, understand, and apply them systematically over time. Your commitment to financial education has equipped you with these same principles, making wealth creation not a matter of luck, but an inevitable result of correct application of proven strategies.

The Wealth Creation Formula

Wealth follows mathematical principles that reward consistency, patience, and strategic thinking over time. Compound interest works identically for everyone regardless of background, social status, or starting capital. Market principles apply universally to those who understand and utilize them correctly.

Your newfound understanding reveals that wealth creation involves identifying and exploiting gaps between value and price, whether in stocks, real estate, businesses, or personal skills that can be developed and monetized through strategic career advancement or entrepreneurial ventures.

The game of wealth has rules that favor those who understand them while disadvantaging those who remain ignorant of these principles. Your education has leveled the playing field by providing access to knowledge that was previously gatekept by financial institutions and wealthy families who preferred to maintain information advantages.

Your Challenge: Transform Knowledge into Action

Knowledge without action remains merely intellectual entertainment—interesting but ultimately powerless to transform your financial reality. The true test of your wealth rebellion journey lies not in what you now know, but in how courageously and consistently you apply this knowledge to create tangible improvements in your financial situation.

Your challenge begins immediately, today, with concrete actions that bridge the gap between aspiration and achievement. These are not suggestions or recommendations, but essential steps that separate those who dream about wealth from those who systematically build it through disciplined, strategic action over time.

The wealth-building journey requires you to overcome the inertia of old habits while developing new patterns of thinking and behaving that align with your expanded understanding of financial opportunity and wealth creation strategies.

Immediate Action Items

Open an investment account today—not tomorrow, not next week, but today. Choose a reputable, low-cost brokerage platform and begin investing immediately, even if you start with just $25. The psychological shift from someone who plans to invest to someone who actively builds wealth through investment begins with your first trade, your first deposit, your first step into the market.

Start a side hustle within the next thirty days that leverages skills you already possess or can quickly develop. This doesn't require a perfect business plan or substantial capital—it requires action that generates income outside your primary employment while building entrepreneurial skills and market understanding that compound over time.

Read your first cryptocurrency whitepaper this week while beginning to understand the technology and economic principles that drive digital asset markets. Whether or not you decide to invest in cryptocurrencies, understanding blockchain technology positions you ahead of those who remain confused by rapidly evolving digital financial systems.

Building Momentum Through Consistent Action

Establish automatic investment systems that ensure consistent wealth building regardless of emotions, market conditions, or competing priorities that might otherwise derail your financial progress through inconsistent contribution patterns.

Network strategically with others who share wealth-building mindsets while avoiding those who reinforce limiting beliefs about money and success that might undermine your commitment to financial transformation and strategic thinking.

Track your net worth monthly while celebrating progress that demonstrates your growing financial strength and provides motivation to continue building wealth through systematic application of wealth creation principles and strategies.

Knowledge is Leverage—And You Now Hold the Blueprint

Information asymmetry has historically been one of the greatest sources of economic inequality, with those possessing superior knowledge extracting value from those operating with incomplete or incorrect information about wealth-building opportunities and financial principles.

You have now eliminated this disadvantage by acquiring comprehensive understanding of investment strategies, business development, real estate opportunities, digital assets, government programs, and financial systems that enable wealth creation across multiple asset classes and income streams.

Your knowledge represents leverage that amplifies every dollar you invest, every hour you work, and every decision you make by ensuring that your efforts align with proven wealth-building principles rather than operating blindly through trial and error that wastes time and resources.

The Power of Informed Decision-Making

Your understanding of compound interest ensures that you recognize the time value of money while making investment decisions that maximize long-term growth rather than seeking immediate gratification that sacrifices future wealth for present consumption.

Knowledge of tax strategies enables you to legally minimize tax burdens while maximizing after-tax returns through strategic use of retirement accounts, business deductions, and investment timing that keeps more wealth in your pocket rather than paying unnecessary taxes.

Understanding of market cycles prevents emotional decision-making during volatility while enabling strategic positioning that capitalizes on opportunities that others miss due to fear, greed, or lack of historical perspective about normal market fluctuations and recovery patterns.

Your Competitive Advantage

Financial literacy provides permanent competitive advantages that compound over time as your knowledge deepens and your experience validates theoretical understanding through practical application and market participation that builds both wealth and wisdom simultaneously.

You now recognize opportunity where others see obstacles, understanding that economic challenges create the best wealth-building opportunities for those positioned to take advantage of dislocations, fear, and temporary market inefficiencies that reward patient capital and strategic thinking.

Your blueprint for wealth creation transcends current economic conditions, political climates, or market trends because it's based on fundamental principles that have created wealth throughout history and will continue creating wealth for those who understand and apply them consistently over time.

The System Wasn't Built for You—But Now You Know How to Beat It

The financial system was indeed designed by and for those who already possessed capital, knowledge, and connections that provided advantages in wealth creation while creating barriers that excluded those without these initial advantages from accessing the same opportunities and pathways to prosperity.

But your journey has revealed a crucial truth: while the system wasn't built for you, it can be conquered by you through superior knowledge, strategic thinking, and persistent action that leverages available opportunities while creating new pathways that serve your wealth-building objectives.

You are no longer subject to the system's limitations because you understand its rules, its weaknesses, and its opportunities well enough to navigate it successfully while building wealth that provides increasing independence from its constraints and requirements.

Beating the System Through Understanding

Traditional gatekeepers lose power when you understand that their services can be bypassed through direct access to markets, information, and opportunities that technology has democratized for anyone willing to learn and act strategically rather than accepting conventional limitations.

Complex financial products designed to extract fees can be avoided through simple, low-cost alternatives that provide better returns while transparent pricing and performance metrics enable informed decision-making that serves your interests rather than enriching intermediaries.

Information asymmetries that once favored institutions are eliminated through your commitment to continuous learning while your growing expertise enables recognition of opportunities and assessment of risks that less-informed participants cannot identify or evaluate accurately.

Your Declaration of Financial Independence

You are no longer dependent on others for your financial future because you possess the knowledge and tools necessary to create wealth through your own informed decisions and strategic actions that align with proven wealth-building principles and opportunities.

Your wealth rebellion has equipped you with the capability to opt out of systems that don't serve you while building alternatives that align with your values and objectives through entrepreneurship, strategic investing, and community building that creates shared prosperity.

The system may not have been built for you, but you have learned to build within it, around it, and beyond it through creativity, persistence, and strategic application of wealth-creation principles that transcend any single economic system or set of rules.

Your Wealth Rebellion Continues

This book ends, but your wealth rebellion has only just begun. You are now armed with knowledge that transforms every day into an opportunity for wealth creation, every challenge into a potential business solution, and every interaction into a chance to build networks that support your long-term financial objectives.

Your rebellion continues with every investment that chooses growth over consumption, every entrepreneurial venture that creates value for others while building wealth for yourself, and every moment you choose strategic thinking over reactive behavior that might compromise your long-term financial success.

The revolution you began by opening this book becomes complete only when you close it and immediately begin applying its lessons to transform your financial reality through concrete actions that demonstrate your commitment to building the wealth and lifestyle you deserve.

The Rebel's Ongoing Mission

Share your knowledge with others who remain trapped by financial ignorance while building communities of mutual support and shared learning that strengthen everyone's wealth-building capabilities through collaboration and collective wisdom.

Continue your education through books, courses, and experiences that deepen your understanding while expanding your capabilities to identify and capitalize on new opportunities as markets evolve and new wealth-creation possibilities emerge.

Measure your success not only by personal wealth accumulation but by the positive impact you create through job creation, community development, and example-setting that inspires others to begin their own wealth rebellion journeys.

Your Legacy Awaits

The wealth you build becomes a foundation for the legacy you leave, creating opportunities for future generations while contributing to community development and social progress through responsible wealth creation and strategic philanthropy.

Your transformation from uninformed to educated, from consumer to creator, from hustler to strategist becomes proof that the wealth rebellion is not just possible but inevitable for those who commit to learning and applying wealth-building principles with consistency and determination.

The system wasn't built for you, but you have learned to beat it, and in doing so, you become part of building a better system—one where knowledge is shared, opportunities are accessible, and wealth creation serves not just individual prosperity but collective advancement toward a more equitable and prosperous society for all.

The revolution begins with the next decision you make. Choose wealth. Choose knowledge. Choose action. Choose rebellion.

The system wasn't built for you—but now you know how to beat it.

Your wealth rebellion starts now.

Chapter 19: The Manifesto: The Rebellion Begins

The chains are broken. The lies are exposed. The system is naked, and you are no longer its prisoner.
But rebellion isn't just about tearing down. It's about what comes next.
Most will stop here. They'll rage, they'll nod, they'll close the book and go back to sleep. But not you.
You've seen too much. You've felt the fracture.
The rebellion doesn't end with breaking. It begins with building.
If you're ready to forge something indestructible, turn the page.
The blueprint awaits.

About the Author

Kenneth Hughes is the founder of KLH Publishing, an architect, and editor. His work dismantles illusions and builds myth shattering systems for readers who refuse to play by the rules. With a background in publishing, design, and accessibility editing, Hughes crafts legacy-driven works that empower readers to reclaim sovereignty—one blueprint at a time.

Available Now: Build Your Legacy

If *Flip the System* broke the illusion, *Build Your Legacy* lays the foundation. Volume Two of *Money Rebellion* shifts from fire to stone—offering tactical systems, rituals, and scalable strategies for wealth that endures. No hacks. No permission. Just sovereignty.

Published by KLH Publishing

This book is part of the *Money Rebellion* series, published by KLH Publishing—an imprint dedicated to emotionally resonant, founder-grade works that empower outsiders to build legacy on their own terms.

If this book has sparked something in you—then share it. Leave a review. Pass it forward. The rebellion grows one reader at a time.

Thank you for reading Money Rebellion: Flip the System.

KLH PUBLISHING

KENNETH HUGHES
AUTHOR

www.ingramcontent.com/pod-product-compliance
Lightning Source LLC
LaVergne TN
LVHW080043210926
848481LV00011B/3269